Fiona Castle

Dying To Live

Fiona Castle Recommends:
Dying To Live

The Christian teaching on life after death

Jim Graham

LEIGH ROAD
BAPTIST CHURCH
ESSEX

Hodder & Stoughton
LONDON SYDNEY AUCKLAND

British Library Cataloguing in Publication Data
A record for this book is available from the British Library

ISBN 0 340 73558 9

Typeset by Avon Dataset Ltd, Bidford-on-Avon, Warks

Printed and bound in Great Britain by
Clays Ltd, St Ives plc

Hodder and Stoughton Ltd
A Division of Hodder Headline PLC
338 Euston Road
London NW1 3BH

Introduction by Fiona Castle

When I was asked by David Moloney of Hodder & Stoughton to re-introduce a book which had been out of print, I had this one in mind before I had even finished reading the letter. I was thrilled when, in a subsequent conversation with David, he said that if I could send him a copy of this book to read, he would consider it. I sent him my only, precious, well-thumbed copy on the promise of its safe return, with the hope that in time it would become readily available once more to those who would benefit from its wisdom.

When I heard some years ago that it was going out of print, I hurriedly bought up six of the remainders. They have since been given, borrowed, lent and not returned!

So why should I be so excited about the re-availability of a book which to some would seem to have a rather morbid title?

There are some books which become dated because of the changes in our society, the enormous and unrelenting advances in technology and by the sheer pressure of life today compared with even two decades ago.

However, God's principles never change. His Word is as relevant today as it was 2000 years ago and it is 'as sharp as a two-edged sword' to those who aim to live by its truth.

Death is a subject which is swept under the carpet in a similar way sex was shunned by the Victorians. Yet it is something that is common to every human being irrespective of race, colour, culture and generation. Most people fear it, many ignore it, we all try to delay its onslaught with pills and potions and tucks and colourings – nevertheless, it is inevitable.

Woody Allen said: 'I'm not afraid of dying, I just don't

want to be around when it happens!' I think we would all tend to agree with those sentiments and perhaps if we are honest we would all like to choose our own death scenario. 'I'd like to be healthy to the last, and die in my sleep with the house tidy and my affairs in order!'

Jim Graham wrote this book some time after my father had died and some time before my mother died. Once I had faced my first experience of death at close quarters, it took on a different meaning. The most common questions people ask are: 'Where are they?', 'Are they happy?' and 'Is there life after death?'

This book sets out to explain the Bible's view of death and life after death; how we can prepare for it and how it can be gained. Furthermore, it teaches us how we can cope with the death of a loved one in a very real way without sentimentality or sweeteners.

I have read other books by Jim Graham and I have been privileged to have known him as Senior Pastor of Gold Hill Baptist Church over many years. I have always admired the way he has taught me not just to learn about God's Word, but to apply its principles directly into my own life and circumstances in a very practical way. What a gift!

As it happened, Jim was ministering communion to my husband, Roy, at his bedside, for the last time before he died. He was witness to Roy, although very weak, sitting up in bed and saying that he saw Jesus standing in the doorway of his bedroom! Roy was a very straightforward, uncomplicated person. He had a simple faith and knew his Saviour, and, I believe, was being prepared to be with Him forever. As Jim says in this book, he was indeed moving from the land of the dying to the land of the living.

Jim shares with us the reality of life after death and the hope that we have in Jesus, and takes the fear out of the grieving process. I thank God for Jim Graham and heartily recommend *Dying to Live*. It is a brilliant read, which should be savoured by everyone. We ignore it at our peril!

Contents

1 So it was true   7

2 Death – Without pretending   19

3 Death – Where is he now?   36

4 Death – But not the end   52

5 Judgment – The bills have to be paid
   sometime   69

6 Hell – The real terror   84

7 Heaven – Home at last!   97

8 Angels – This home has servants too!   113

9 There are so many questions   126

10 Bereavement – Please, may I have
   permission to cry?   141

To all those who having died are now living, but who in their lives influenced and affected my life so deeply.

Acknowledgements

I am grateful to so many who have opened their hearts and shared their lives with me as they approached the experience of dying, and others as they faced the reality of bereavement. My thanks is due too to Dr Joan Dalton for supplying material for the first chapter of this book; to Miss Pam Kerr for her willing and enthusiastic typing and correcting of the MSS; and especially to Anne, my wife, for her patience with me and encouragement to me as I wrote.

1: So it was true

Towards the close of his life, Professor T. H. Huxley, the eminent Victorian scientist who invented the term 'agnostic' and applied it to himself, went through a period of intense mental and spiritual illumination which led to the swift reversal of the judgments of a lifetime. The nurse who was responsible for caring for him during the last weeks of his life tells us that shortly before he died, a dazzling revelation of the reality of the Unseen seemed to break in suddenly and dramatically upon him. Raising himself on his elbows, his eyes which had been dulled now sparkling and his pale face now glowing, he gazed transported for a few moments on some invisible scene. Then, as the pageant seemed to fade, he sank back on his pillows, murmuring wistfully: 'So it was true!'

Such a vision is not given to all. From time to time I have known those who in their own way have stood momentarily on the tall, sunlit peaks of hope, their gaunt faces aflame with the glow of an immortal dawn, their spirits braced and stirred by the eternal winds of God, but for most it seems that entrance to the land of the living from the land of the dying is secured by walking in the shadows of the valley rather than the glory of the mountain peaks.

A few are comforted by the fact that death is a night which has no morning. Charles Swinburne, the English poet, puts it in this way:

From too much love of living,
From hope and fear set free,
We thank with brief thanksgiving
Whatever gods may be
That no life lives for ever;

That dead men rise up never;
That even the weariest river
Winds somewhere safe to sea.

Others find peace in the fact that 'after labour comes rest; after struggle, peace; after life's fitful fever, this last sleep.' Lord Byron testifies to the response in his own heart: 'I see no horror in a dreamless sleep, and I have no conception of any existence which duration would not make tiresome.' Many, however, feel after the reality of life after death which is based not on the feelings of sentiment, but on the facts of the Scriptures of God, sensing that a human verdict is not adequate in these circumstances, but that there is a need for an authoritative word by One who is able to give it. So in the eighteenth century Isaac Watts wrote:

There is a land of pure delight,
Where saints immortal reign;
Infinite day excludes the night,
And pleasures banish pain;

There everlasting spring abides,
And never-withering flowers;
Death, like a narrow sea divides
This heavenly land from ours.

But timorous mortals start and shrink
To cross this narrow sea,
And linger shivering on the brink,
And fear to launch away.

O could we make our doubts remove,
Those gloomy doubts that rise,
And see the Canaan that we love
With unbeclouded eyes.

However we may consider death, approximately two-thirds of a million people die each year in the United Kingdom. That means two-thirds of a million families are affected to some greater or lesser degree by the presence of death. Death is one of the constantly and often unexpectedly intruding facts into our lives. It is foolish to refuse to think about it or even to pretend it does not exist, for sooner or later it will bestraddle the pathway of our lives and ask the question, 'What do you think of me?'

As far as I can remember my first encounter with death was the death of my grandmother. She had been ill for some considerable time, and I was aware of how serious her condition was, not by anything which I was told, but by the pain which I noticed on the faces of some of my close relatives, and the whispered urgency with which her illness was spoken of. My enquiries about her were met by replies which never seemed to measure up to the atmosphere of adult conversation. She died, and one of my abiding memories of the last weeks of her life is that she had a box of chocolate finger biscuits which she kept by her bedside, and I was given one from time to time. The other memory that remains of that time is that the minister of our church was constantly commended in private family conversations for his faithfulness in visiting her—although, I recollect, he came in for some considerable criticism in almost every other area of his ministry. I liked him, and, in a childish way, I was glad that he obviously managed to do something well. Where there had been a great deal of activity, and I had known a lot of fun in that home, there was now stillness, emptiness, and the blinds were drawn until the funeral was over. The coffin was placed awesomely in the bedroom and adults were sometimes invited to go in there to inspect it. The day of the funeral was a bitterly cold day (or did I just think it was a bitterly cold day?), and again the minister did very well!

My next encounter with death was at school. The Junior Sports Champion had appendicitis and I understood them to say that his appendix had 'burst' and this led to his quite unexpected death. When I first heard this I could not believe that it had happened – and it haunted me for weeks. I was comforted by the fact that a Junior Sports Champion Memorial Cup was thereafter presented annually to his memory, and as far as I know it still is at my old school. I remember feeling that that was right and fitting and as far as I can remember I willingly contributed to a fund which made the purchase of this Memorial Cup possible. I had a sense of pride that I had known him – although not really very well.

The main-line encounter was still to come. It was announced one evening (I sensed with some awkwardness, if not embarrassment) that my Mother had been that morning to see our Doctor, and as a result needed to go to Hospital on the following morning 'to have an operation'. The lack of detail and the matter-of-factness with which this information was conveyed betrayed that all was not well. The 'operation' took place, and the first visit I made to the Hospital was quite devastating. I had never seen anyone quite so ill before and it reminded me of my grandmother. The next two years are deeply etched in my mind – the gradually deteriorating body of someone I loved very much; the pain which she had, which sometimes appeared to be quite unbearable; the Hospital treatment which she underwent which often left her wretched; the shock of discovering she was dying; the embargo that was put on any attempt to talk about the fact she was dying to her or to anyone else; the necessity to have my dog 'put down' because the time came when he would not allow our family doctor to go near her; her eventual death in hospital in the early hours of one Monday morning; my return home early that morning to discover that strangely our home had become a house since I had left on the evening of the previous day; the coldness of my bed; the warmth of the September sun three days later at the graveside; the many expressions of kindness and help; the subsequent collapse of my Christian faith; the loneliness; the bereftness; the aching longing that somebody somehow would put the clock back and the events of the past two years could be avoided on the re-run of life.

The years passed and my faith was restored. I became a minister – and consequently as I pastored a congregation I faced the reality of death on a regular basis in a multitude of circumstances. It came to the old and it came to the young; sometimes it was peaceful and sometimes agonising to watch; it intruded with unexpected suddenness and then again it could linger in a painfully protracted way through long days and much longer nights – all calling for some realistic acknowledgement. Some of these encounters inevitably have been quite outstanding for a variety of reasons and my memory recalls them in quite remarkable detail. None more so than that of Andrew, who had left school at the age of 11; lived his life through many overwhelming difficulties; was on his way to commit suicide in the River Leven when he was apprehended by Jesus Christ and became a Christian. These were early days in my life as a minister and I discovered that through the subsequent years of his life he learned a great deal about the Bible and he was willing to share many insights with me. I discovered one day with a great deal of sadness in my heart, that Andrew was dying. The day before he died I visited him in hospital, and he beckoned me to come down close to him to hear what he wanted to say to me. To my great joy he said: 'They will tell you I am sinking. Don't believe them, I am rising.' So Andrew departed to be with the Lord.

I remember interviewing a Christian doctor in one of our Sunday church services and asking him what differences he had observed in Christians and non-Christians as they were in the process of dying. He replied with a disarming frankness that in his experience occasionally there was a very marked difference, but often there was not. In the full health of life we often say and sing the right things, but faced with the stark reality of death these verbal convictions

11

crumble. There is a cultural conclusion that death is the final tragedy and we respond accordingly. Whether this is the result of our cultural environment or whether there are even more significant reasons for this reaction I find it hard to say. This is why Gertrude Knevels found it necessary to express something which many of us find hard to grasp:

Shall I wear mourning for my soldier dead,
I – a believer? Give me red,
Or give me royal purple for the King
At whose high court my love is visiting.
Dress me in green for growth, for life made new
For skies his dear feet march, dress me in blue,
In white for his dear soul; robe me in gold
For all the pride that his new rank shall hold.
In earth's dim gardens blooms no hue too bright
To dress me for my love who walks in light.

When someone dies it is very natural and healthy to be sad; but what we ought always to remember is that at such a time our sorrow is for ourselves, and not for those who have died. It is they who are really alive if they truly died in Christ. So far from being sorry we ought to be glad that they have left the land of the dying and entered the land of the living. In the early Church the Christian martyrs called the day of their death their 'birth-day'. John Ruskin once said: 'I will not wear black for the guests of God'. One of the incomprehensible things in life is that even as Christians we wear the colour of deepest gloom in honour of those who have entered into the greatest glory. The appearances of death and the culture in which we live persuade us at a very deep level, often quite irrationally, that what we believe as Christians is not true. We cannot banish sorrow – nor should we – when those we love die, but we can at least be sure that our sorrow is not for them, but for ourselves if the one who has died has responded to the reality of Jesus Christ, Who said 'I am the Resurrection and the Life. He who believes in Me will live, even though he dies; and whoever lives and believes in Me will never die'.

Great interest has been generated in more recent years in the reality that whatever it is, death is not the end. The *Sun* in the early weeks of January, 1977, ran a series of main-line articles on life after death. It clearly indicated that some people believe there is life after death, and some do not. But it cited another group of people who claimed to *know* that there is life after death. These are people who according to some medical definitions of death have 'died' – sometimes more than once. They then have the process of death reversed and come back to tell of their experiences. This newspaper provided a number of 'case-histories' or testimonies to this event. It also referred to an American scientist, Dr Raymond A. Moody, Jnr, who has talked to dozens of people who claim to have experienced death. He discovered that there were fifteen factors which repeatedly cropped up in these testimonies. Most people experienced at least eight of these factors, but many recalled as many as twelve. Talking about his study about the life-after-death experience, Dr Moody said: 'I have tried to be as objective and straightforward as I can, but my background, opinions and prejudices inevitably come into it.' That certainly would seem to be an honest appraisal of the scientist as a human being. He claims that he did not set out to prove that there is life after death since he does not think that such scientific proof is yet possible, but he urges: 'all I ask is for anyone who disbelieves what he reads here to poke around a bit for himself. Many who have done so have come to share my bafflement over these events.' There are certain inherent dangers in 'poking around' in the area of death and we will look at this a little later on, but the danger should not deter us from an honest awareness and concern about the realities that lie there. The *Sun* on its centre page spread set out the fifteen faces of death most frequently experienced.

Space

No real-life words can describe it and so consequently it is

13

difficult, if not impossible, to convey. As one woman said: 'Our world is three-dimensional, but the next one definitely is not. I have to describe it to you in words that are three-dimensional. That is as close as I can get. But it is not really adequate.'

Fearless

Almost every survivor claims to *be unafraid* of death – although none would say he wanted to die before his time.

Words

Many heard their doctor or others pronounce them dead. One woman heard her doctor say as he tried to resuscitate her because of heart failure: 'Let's try one more time and then we'll give up.' On that last time she responded. She told her doctor that she did not remember much about her 'death', but she did hear him say: 'Let's try one more time and then we'll give up.'

Music

Strange, and sometimes unpleasant, sounds seem to fill the head. It has been described as like loud buzzing, ringing, roaring, banging. One man heard, however, what sounded like Japanese wind-bells, whilst a woman described: 'a majestic, really beautiful sort of music.'

Speed

Often, at the same time as the noise, people felt they were being pulled at great speed through a dark space. It is described as a cave, a trough, an enclosure, a tunnel, a funnel, a vacuum, a void, a sewer, a valley or a cylinder.

Floating

At the end of the dark tunnel, a dying person often finds he is looking down on his own body, as if he is floating above it.

Spirits

Other spiritual beings sometimes come to the dying person to help him on his journey out of life. Or sometimes to tell him to go back because his time has not come. Often, these spirits are recognised as loved ones who have died.

Light
A being of light, more dazzling than the eyes could stand in life, is the most amazing element of the death experience. It radiates love, and commands the dying, without use of words, to evaluate their lives. Christians mostly identify the light as Christ. But even a man with no religious training or beliefs identified 'the being of light'.

Flashback
An instant review of a whole life-time, in fast visual images, passes before the dying person. He may even re-live the emotions felt at the time of the events.

Border
A border or limit – like a fence, a stretch of water, a mist or even just a line – features in a few near-deaths. The person seems to be approaching it, and sometimes sees the other side. But he rarely crosses it.

Contented
Once the person has gone far enough on the trip away from the living, there is no desire to return. This is so especially where there has been an encounter with the 'being of light'.

Realism
Once a person has returned to life, he tells what happened as a real series of events. It has impressed upon him that this is not an experience like a dream in any of its elements.

Loving
Survivors of death all claim it has a deep influence on their lives (in the light of the preceding characteristics that would seem to be at least understandable!). Mostly they want to love others more. They describe a thirst for knowledge and a need to learn. They do not feel purified in any way.

Peaceful
Feelings of extreme comfort, peace and quiet are often felt at the beginning of a temporary death. This is so even when the person is severely or violently injured.

Witnesses
A lot of the details of a person's 'death' can be checked out with people who were there when it happened. Events

which have been 'watched' by somebody who has 'left his body' match up amazingly with living witnesses' versions of the same scene.

This investigation has all the marks of personal 'eye-witness' testimony, which make clinical precision difficult, but press upon us a vital factor in reality. If a dead person is resuscitated, it can be argued that they never were dead. Dr Moody would spontaneously agree that 'by this definition, none of my cases would qualify', However, some of Dr Moody's cases were 'dead' for up to twenty minutes, and this would normally be thought to be beyond the limits of resuscitation.

A young housewife in her early thirties suddenly collapsed with a heart attack. She apparently sensed, by one means or another, that she was dying. She says: 'I found myself in a black void. I know I had left my physical body behind. I thought, "God, I did the best I know how. Please help me!" Immediately, I was moved out of that blackness through a pale grey. I just went on gliding swiftly. In the distance I could see a grey mist, and I was rushing towards it. Beyond the mist I could see people and buildings. The whole thing was permeated with the most gorgeous light. It was a living, golden yellow glow. It was such a wonderful, joyous feeling. Yet it was not my time to go through the mist. From the other side, my Uncle Carl, who had died many years earlier, appeared. He blocked my path and said: "Go back! Your work on earth has not been completed."Straightaway, I was back in my body. I felt that horrible pain in my chest, and I heard my little boy crying, "God, bring my mummy back to me."' (the *Sun* Thursday, January 27, 1977.) I have recorded this as it stands without comment. However, such a testimony raises huge and serious issues for the scientist, the humanist, and the Christian alike. Nevertheless it does reinforce the conclusion in 'The Undiscovered Country' (*British Medical Journal* 15th December, 1979) that '. . . doubts about the possibility of some form of life after death remain to puzzle only the sceptics and the agnostics.' It also challenges the conclusion of Bertrand Russell, who can only say: 'No fire, no heroism, no intensity of thought or feeling can preserve an individual life beyond the grave; that all the labours of the ages, all the devotions, all the inspiration, all the noonday brightness of human genius, are destined to extinction in the vast death of the solar system, and that the whole temple of man's achievement must inevitably be buried beneath the debris of a universe in ruins.' It seems to dismiss any suggestion that Robert Browning's description 'God took him to Himself, as you would lift a sleeping child from a dark uneasy bed into your arms and the light' is simply a poet's fancy trying to ease the smart and pain of an intolerable grief and cover up the grim facts with the protective camouflage of an illusion.

Dr Eugene Brodey found it necessary to defend his decision, as Editor of the *Journal of Nervous and Mental Diseases*, to devote a whole issue of it in 1977 to the paranormal, re-incarnation, and the evidence of man's survival after death. In that publication material was surveyed from accounts taken from people involved in climbing accidents who expected to die but escaped (*Psychiatry* 1976 by R. Noyes and R. Kletti); experiences recorded from people after cardiac arrest (R. G. Druss and D. S. Kornfield in the *Journal of the American Medical Association* 1967; T. G. Hackett, N. H. Cassem, and H. A. Wishnie in the *New England Journal of Medicine* 1968; and M. Dobson in the *British Medical Journal* 1971); and other near-fatal illnesses (R. Noyes and others in the *Journal of Nervous and Mental Diseases* 1977; and M. B. Sabom and S. Kreutziger in the *Journal of the Florida Medical Association* 1977); and stories of the rare people who have survived suicidal jumps from the Golden Gate Bridge in San Francisco (D. H. Rosen in the *Western Journal of Medicine* 1975).

Dr I. Stevenson and Dr D. Greyson in the *Journal of the American Medical Association* were able to identify some

17

common features which agree with the fifteen faces of death which have already been mentioned. They conclude that the striking agreement in the reports from people in different countries and cultures and in different decades encourages the belief that valid conclusions can be drawn from them. With typical scientific hesitation they advocate caution in view of the possible suggestion on the part of the interviewed (whether enthusiastic or sceptical), and the subtle communication from other survivors in one way or another. They are concerned lest the published and broadcast accounts of others' experiences may all play a part in exaggerating any apparent conformity in survivors' accounts. They are also at pains to point out that these accounts are – by definition scientifically – near-death experiences and depend, as far as science can judge, on a functioning and not a dead brain. Dr R. Noyes in *Psychiatry* (1972) makes an astonishingly categorical statement for a scientist that 'no-one has returned from the dead and given an account of his experiences.' No doubt he is persuaded by a conclusion which Shakespeare expresses in *Hamlet* that death remains

> the undiscover'd country from whose bourn
> No traveller returns . . .

In the article 'The Undiscovered Country' in the *British Medical Journal* the writer concludes 'the near dead are not dead; and the dead, whether surviving in some form or not, can be left to thanatology and eschatology.' It is to this that we now turn to explore, not on the basis of human sentiment (which expresses itself persistently and very volubly even in the most rational and sensitive), or the groping conclusions of science, but on the revealed heart of God in the Bible. As we explore together there will always be a consciousness that what we are looking at is not something remote and academic, but something intensely personal which demands honest answers to significant questions.

2: Death – Without pretending

Death intrudes upon our lives in a multitude of ways, although the past century has seen the taming and the eliminating of many past killers. Disease heads the list of the number of guises in which it comes. Typhus, smallpox and diphtheria are among those that no longer claim their quota of lives as they used to – at least in countries where modern medicine and hygiene are able to be practised and observed. However, these have been replaced by diseases which are closely related to the problem areas of modern life – pollution, stress, diet and insufficient physical activity.

In an era when technology has advanced out of all recognition and machinery has resulted which is not only more widespread, but faster and more complicated, and transport has become unbelievably more rapid, accidental death has also increased.

Perhaps the outstanding guise of death in our time, however, is the phenomenon of mass killing. The mass bombing and resulting obliteration of whole cities in World War II culminating in the atomic destruction of Nagasaki and Hiroshima introduced a new phase of death to our civilisation. Genocide, although not entirely new in human history, achieved a new notoriety in the extermination of six million Jews in the Nazi holocaust.

At this time when law and order has become a top priority for Western politicians the whole frightening development of acts of violence is a stark reality which stares us threateningly in the face. The ready availability of the gun which insulates a killer against personal contact with those he kills – feeling their flesh; smelling their body odour; etc. – provides a coward's advantage, and is a considerable factor in the increase.

However, death is death, whether by cancer in ancient Egypt or in the Royal Marsden Hospital in London; whether by a stone catapult or an ounce of metal exploding in a Robert F. Kennedy's head or a Martin Luther King's neck; whether by crushing under chariot wheels on the Appian Way or by impact from the best part of a ton of mechanised metal on the M1; whether by starvation in a besieged city long-since sunk into oblivion or obliteration by a hydrogen bomb.

The electroencephalogram may replace a mirror held before the mouth; and the heart monitor may replace the uncertain attempts to locate a pulse beat in the wrist or neck. Resuscitation methods may become less and less crude and the mask and oxygen cylinder may replace mouth to mouth procedure. Post-mortems may well become more and more sophisticated and cosmetic embalming may take the place of putting pennies on the eyelids. The black-bordered undertakers advertisement in the local paper may be replaced by a solemn little song on local radio:

Chambers caskets are just fine
Made of sandalwood and pine.
If your loved ones have to go,
Ring Columbus 5-4-0.

Everything may change – but death remains changeless. We may soften its horror by 'paying our last respects' to a corpse. We may patch it up, preserve it, dress it in going-away clothes; give it a hair-do; surround it with flowers; disguise its final grave with artificial grass or its cremation bier with subdued and tasteful lighting – but disposing of the body with grace and sensitivity either by burying or burning does not provide a satisfying answer to the penetrating questions asked by the mystery and the reality of death. We are unable to beautify death however hard we try. We may learn to live with it, and come to accept it, but we cannot change it. Death destroys beauty. Few of us can have driven on the lanes, arterial roads and motorways of our country, without a passing thought for the masses of unrecognisable fur and mangled flesh that lie there, all cold and motionless and offensive. One moment that animal was graceful, beautiful, flying, singing, scurrying, burrowing; the next moment awfully dead. There is something – even in the animal world which is so unnatural, grotesque, and even wrong, about death. Violent death creates obscenity – tasteless, horrid and raw.

In the Bible Job mobilises it: 'He is torn from the security of his tent and marched off to the king of terrors'; the Psalmist verbalises it: 'My heart is in anguish within me; the terrors of death assail me'. The writer to the Hebrews lays its true character bare when he speaks of Jesus freeing those 'who all their lives were held in slavery by their fear of death'.

Yet we erect around it a conspiracy of silence which is almost a denial of death. We are so critical of the Victorians because they sentimentalised death and surrounded it with pathos. For the Victorians the public discussion (and even mention!) of sex was taboo, but we have reversed this attitude to death and sex in our culture. The language we use when we can do no other than face death gives the lie to our embarrassment. We speak of a person having 'passed away' or 'left us' or 'has gone now' or 'slipped off' or 'passed on'. The word 'died' seems to stick in our throat. One Sunday afternoon while I was preparing to share in the first Sunday Evening Service of a new year, the telephone rang in my office. The accent of the caller was familiar, but the voice was not. Once I had established his identity (he had never called me before!) I was alarmed to learn that his mother had been involved in an accident that morning. She had been in her car alone; the car had skidded on black ice; the police had been involved; the car was very badly damaged; the word 'instantaneous' had been used – and hung like a cloud of fear in the air. He could not bring himself to use the word 'killed' or 'dead' – nor could I! What seemed like an endless conversation (although it only lasted a few minutes) pumped adrenalin into my body as it gradually dawned on me that he was phoning to tell me that a very dear friend, who had encouraged and prayed for me over many years in the ministry, was dead. Even now it seems so unreal – like a dream that has no substance. But hesitancy to use the word to describe and communicate the reality did not alter the fact of the matter – she was dead!

Even in the Church these days we do not hear too many sermons on death. It used to be spoken of often from the pulpit in graphic detail in the late part of the last century, and the early part of this one. But this is no longer so. To check the index of our hymn books is to become aware that this is no longer a common theme.

When death is seriously presented on the media (as in the Theatre of the Absurd) it is ridiculed as a cosmic joke, or defined as a meaningless accident in a meaningless universe.

Since death is so obviously real and certain why not prepare for it carefully and honestly? It was Socrates who observed that, 'the essence of philosophy is preparation for death'. When we have to make a journey, making preparation for departure neither brings it nearer nor delays it. But the day of departure is much more orderly and peaceful as a result. We were involved personally with a member of our fellowship some years ago who was setting out for the Far East as a missionary. There was an enormous amount of preparation involved – the basic customs of the new culture had to be investigated; the climate had to be acknowledged and clothes and equipment chosen accordingly; arrangements had to be finalised for storing what had to be left behind; medical procedures had to be gone through to make sure that sufficient protection was given against potentially hazardous diseases in the new environment; all the paraphernalia of trans-continental travel had to be checked – passport, visa, medical authorisation, tickets, stop-overs; plane times; check-in times; baggage; etc. All of this preparation – and she would be returning in a maximum of four years time, and potentially could return at any time! Beside death this, and even moon landings and space travel, pale in significance.

Dr Cicely Saunders, of St Christopher's Hospice, London, which cares almost exclusively for the terminally ill, says that as people face the reality of death with honesty and prepare for departure from this life, it is the time when they can be emotionally and psychologically most mature. She alludes to the late Pope John who said: 'My bags are packed. I am ready to leave.' Her concept of one of the main functions of the Hospice is that they are helping patients to pack their bags – each in his own individual way, and making his own choices. While there is a reluctance in most of us to pack our bags for any trip, even if only to go on holiday, none of us would deny it is essential to do so.

Fear is the dominating reaction when we think of and face up to the reality of death. Indeed Dr Paul Tillich, the theologian, in his book, *The Courage to Be* points out that there are three dominant elements in the deep underlying anxiety which characterises our culture in the latter part of the twentieth century. First, there is a sense of blank meaninglessness from which the soul recoils in horror – a kind of what-does-it-matter-anyway attitude to life. Life has no purpose or significance and is heading aimlessly for nothing. It all adds up to the same thing in the end – nothing. Secondly, says Tillich, there is a deep ineradicable sense of guilt in human nature to which all the great literature of the world bears witness. It issues in a feeling of foreboding and suppressed apprehension, because I have not made of life or myself what I ought to have or could have. Thirdly, there is the fear of death. We are not so preoccupied with the brevity of life as our fathers were, but underneath our careless devil-may-care attitudes this latent dread lurks, conditioning not only our individual behaviour, but also our everyday social conventions. The common practice among doctors of concealing from a dying man the fact of his impending death is one of the evidences of this.

There are normally three ways in which we, as human beings, react to things generally which we fear. We criticise them strongly; laugh at them both in public and in private; and thirdly we pretend that they do not exist. Because we have pretended so much about death, comfort has become a lost art—except for choosing a 'sympathy' card. Let's look at some of the reasons why people fear death.

1. *We are too comfortable here on earth*

Although we grumble and complain about the hardships of life created by economic pressures, relationship difficulties, social inconveniences, politital injustices, and the like, we still find life here too good for the most part to consider leaving it. The vast majority of us in the Western world have very much more than our grandparents had to make life softer and easier and richer. We forget quickly the many hardships with which our forebears had to struggle even at the beginning of this century (and much later!).

Dr Samuel Johnson was being shown around a fine stately home and its grounds and eventually he commented: 'These are the things that make it difficult to die'. It is not that most of us experience that stately home dimension of life here on earth, but there has been a vast improvement in the facilities to take the backache and frustration out of life. It is not that the Bible condemns our having material possessions, but it does warn about the anaesthetising influence which they can have upon us. There is an unwritten saying of Jesus: 'The world is a bridge. The foolish man builds his house upon it. The wise man travels over it'. That is why it is written down that Jesus strongly taught: 'Invest in heaven! Do not hoard treasures on earth where they will decay and fizzle out anyway!'

2. We no longer believe in the reality of things which we cannot see, touch, or investigate

Eddington in 'Science and the Unseen World' says: 'We are no longer tempted to condemn the spiritual aspects of our nature as illusory because of their lack of concreteness. We have travelled far from the standpoint which identifies the real with the concrete'.

Eddington may well have been a brilliant scientist, but as a sociologist he has made a faulty diagnosis. There is a widespread disbelief in anything which you cannot see or investigate by scientific or technological means. It is considered naïve and simplistic to approach life otherwise. There is ample evidence that we live in a culture pretty well dominated by materialism and humanism. A TV poll some years ago indicated that 65 per cent of British people no longer believe in any other life after death. Again, some years ago, a journalist declared: 'Forty years ago the British people stopped believing in hell; twenty years ago the British people stopped believing in heaven.'

Great fear is generated by approaching nothingness – like a night that has no morning and a sunset that has no dawn. Tom Stoppard in *Rosencrantz and Guildenstern are Dead* puts it in a quite terrifying way:

Death is not anything . . . death is not . . .
It's the absence of presence, nothing more . . .
The endless time of never coming back.
A gap you can't see, and when the wind blows through
it it makes no sound.

3. We do not like to face up realistically to disturbing ideas

Death is only one among a whole range of disturbing ideas. Many others are brought into our living rooms and our leisure – hunger, disease, war, poverty, dictatorship, injustice, greed. However powerfully they are presented to us we either switch off eventually or 'put it over' to the Big Match or 'The Good Old Days'. The analysis of a Russian dissident giving almost a prophetic warning, the severe implications of an uncontrolled nuclear arms race, the grim spectacle of pot-bellied children in the Third World, the seemingly undeniable and never-ending political intrigue, all distress us only momentarily, before we turn to the more pressing problems of an oil leak in the car and the need to fit a draught excluder to the window. Fear makes us react in an unusual way to fact.

4. *None of us likes to end a relationship*

This has always been one of our deepest reasons for our fear of death. We were never created to be permanently alone. We are basically social beings, we find fulfilment in the company of others. From the beginning God set the solitary in families and through history the most cruel punishment that human beings can inflict on one another is solitary confinement. Through the experience of living most of us find meaningful, satisfying, significant, creative, tender, strong, enjoyable relationships. These are almost infinite in variety and vary greatly in degree of intensity, but all contribute vastly to the reality of living. The thought of terminating some or all of them is too painful to contemplate.

5. *We do not like the nature of death itself*

Very often death is preceded by weakness – often physical and sometimes mental. One of the costs of more sophisticated medical and technological advances, is that the process of dying is prolonged, even though they have calmed some of death's agonies and deadened some of its pain. This has sometimes created a situation where there is a loss of dignity in dying. Perhaps dying never was, and never could be dignified – its very nature involves humiliation. However, the humiliation appears to be paraded by catheters and bottles, electronic devices and many other aspects of medical emergency. I want to pay my own personal tribute to the kindness and sensitivity of medical personnel in many parts of the country. On many occasions I have sat beside a recently bereaved relative in the Sister's Office by the side of a hospital ward, and again and again I have marvelled at the tenderness and personal concern which have been quite clearly demonstrated – even at times of the day and night when preoccupation with other responsibilities might have caused it to be otherwise. Nevertheless, as others have looked on at the process of dying it has subconsciously made a deep and lasting impression, and resulted in an apprehension over the circumstances which surround it.

This is not death, however, but the process of dying. While closely and inextricably related they are separate issues. It is rather like the relationship which exists between a wedding and a marriage. There is a constant tendency to be preoccupied with the wedding – and neglect the reality which it initiates. Our society has paid dearly, and is reaping a fearful harvest from a Church and clergy who have paid a great deal of attention to the wedding and have spent little time on considering carefully and instructing clearly on the fundamental principles of marriage. So we must press in further beyond the circumstances of dying and ask the question: 'What is the nature of death?'.

a. It is a new experience
John Betjeman, in one of his intriguing poems describes his thoughts before an operation. He is lying in a hospital in Oxford, listening to the tolling of St Giles' bells:

Intolerably sad, profound
St Giles' bells are ringing round . . .
Swing up! and give me hope of life,
Swing down! and plunge the surgeon's knife.
I, breathing for a moment, see
Death wing himself away from me
And think, as on this bed I lie
Is it extinction when I die? . . .

St Giles' bells are asking now
   'And hast thou known the Lord, hast thou?'
St Giles' bells, they richly ring
   'And was that Lord our Christ and King?'
St Giles' bells they hear me call
   'I never knew the Lord at all . . .'

He goes on in this poem called 'Before the Anaesthetic', or 'A Real Fright':

   'Now, lying in the gathering mist
   I know that Lord did not exist;
   Now, lest this "I" should cease to be,
   Come, real Lord, come quick to me . . .
   Almighty Saviour, had I faith,
   There'd be no fight with kindly Death . . .'

There is all the uncertainty, the apprehension, the hesitancy of a man facing a new and real experience. Like a bridegroom on the eve of his marriage or a student on the eve of his Finals, or the short-listed candidate sitting in the waiting-room, waiting for his call to interview – so is the one contemplating death honestly and realistically as a part of life.

b. It is a lonely experience

Martin Heidegger, the philosopher, comments that, 'death is something which no one can do for another'. No one can take your place nor go with you into the experience. Indeed, another phenomenon of our modern culture is that we have often heightened the experience of 'aloneness' as part of death. In past years death was often accompanied by the tender ministrations of loving hands and familiar surroundings. This is not so much so today as death has been banished from home and relocated in hospital. There it is faced in a setting of sterile equipment and efficient and, although frequently tender and sensitive, unfamiliar

28

people. The inherent loneliness of dying has become even more lonely today. Perhaps this is yet another price-tag that has to be reckoned with, attached to medical and technological advance.

To this reality the Christian Gospel responds with a personal conviction from the Psalmist's heart, 'Even when walking through the dark valley of death, I will not be afraid, for you are close beside me guarding, guiding all the way.' The Christian who is dying is accompanied!

c. It is a final experience

This is really where the fear of death originates. Death is a reminder that life is over – the time of my control is gone, and the opportunity for me to make decisions and exercise my will is past. Few, if any, realistically reach the end of life without some regrets and some twinges of a conscience which began to form properly as a child of ten or eleven before puberty. Death presents the challenge of a completed life. Carl Jung, the Swiss psychologist, observes: 'The question of the meaning and worth of life never becomes more urgent or more agonising than when we see the final breath leave a body which a moment before was living.' How awesome is that moment! To observe it is to be aware of its crisis. The time of sowing is over, and the time of reaping has come! Just suppose that all the time the Bible in fact was right – in the next life justice does apply in perfection even though it did not apply in this one. The bills may not have to be paid at the end of each month – but they have to be paid! Here, indeed, we are touching the deepest spring in the fear of death. If there was no life after death then fear of death would be reduced. We may continue to dislike it, and want to postpone it, but not fear it if:

One thing is certain and the rest is lies;
The flower that once has blown, forever dies.

The fear of death finds its origin in the reality that we are facing our lives – we are now being called to account for the way we have lived.

How important it is, then, that we face up to this reality we call death without pretending. Death has been so grossly misrepresented and misunderstood. Man has fumbled in the dark in every generation – possibly because in his heart he has not wanted a proper understanding of death on the basis that 'where ignorance is bliss 'tis folly to be wise'.

As a result he has often said vaguely a number of things about death which are inaccurate.

1. *Death is not real*

However incredible and bizarre this may seem, it has been a conviction held by a number. They believe that death is something in the mind only – it doesn't really happen! Personally, I find this not only unacceptable, but quite offensive in the presence of the bereaved. It insults the intelligence, confuses the broken heart, and denies the facts of the matter.

2. *Life continues after death only in our children; or in the memory; or in the work we have done*

Our hope of survival after death lies only in the influence we have had in this present life and in the impact we have made on it. It is because of this that a proverb has emerged out of Chinese culture: 'There are only four things worth doing in life – planting a tree; writing a book; building a house; and having a son.' The rest is extinction, oblivion and darkness. These are the only things that live on after you have died.

It is true that often we do leave something behind us for good or ill after we have departed this life – but death brings something much more positive than that.

3. *Death is the end*

For eight years we lived in Fifeshire in Scotland. These were happy years spent in a very lovely part of that country.

The Kingdom of Fife is a county of many contrasts – land and sea; mountain and glen; moorland and rich, arable farmland – bounded at its northern and southern parts by the River Tay and the River Forth. In the heart of that county – beneath its soil – lies one of the richest coalfields in the country. Generations of men have spent their lives, and sometimes given their lives, digging in the darkness to produce fuel for industry and home. I remember standing one bleak, wintry afternoon in a hillside cemetery in the coal-producing part of Fife in that awkward, unique moment of bewilderment when the burial service is over waiting for someone to make the first move when an old Fife miner – whom I had never met before – accosted me with forthright antagonism and bitterness and said bluntly: 'Minister, you are wrong! When we die we are buried like a dog in a hole, and that's it!' Is it? Is this sodden, dark, comfortless hole in the ground the terminus? Those who say so are forced to the conclusion that heaven and hell are what you make of life now. Circumstances will dictate your experience. Unfortunately – or perhaps fortunately – we are not in control of our own destiny.

4. Re-incarnation will follow death

This belief declares that there was a previous existence and there will be a subsequent existence – not necessarily in the same form as we experience it now. Although this has a stronger grip in the East, the more frequent mingling of East and West in a multi-racial, multi-faith society has brought a more widespread belief in and popularity to re-incarnation. It brings its own moral challenge in that we need to be careful how we live now since that will determine how we return later.

5. The body has no longer any part to play

Admittedly death very persuasively seems to dispense with the body altogether. However carefully we may treat it after death, in our heart of hearts we are increasingly aware of its

31

deterioration and its ultimate decomposition and disintegration.

The news media at this very moment is giving full coverage to the discovery of human remains in the garden of a home in North London. As 30 police cadets from the Police Training School in Hendon sift through the soil meticulously they are discovering fragments of bone. The pathologists estimate that it is likely from what they have found that a considerable number of people have been interred there. They pursue their macabre profession with extraordinary confidence, with material which to the rest of us is a guarantee of depersonalised anonymity.

Man has concluded in the face of this kind of evidence that some insubstantial, ethereal part of him may indeed persist, but when he dies he is certainly finished with his body. The soul may continue in some kind of disembodied existence, but there is no future for his body.

6. *Universalism*

Many have come to terms with the love of God and have concluded (wrongly as we shall see!) that everybody, without exception, will go to a 'better' place.

While this answers a few difficult questions and could bring some comfort to anxious hearts, nevertheless it raises a whole range of other questions which are equally difficult to deal with. For example it challenges the very heart of human existence, the reality of personal freedom. Again, it presupposes that it does not really matter whether you are a Nero or a St Paul; an Adolf Eichman or an Albert Schweitzer; an Adolf Hitler or a Martin Niemöller; an agnostic or an Augustine; a treacherous Judas or a martyred James – we will all end up much better off than we are now.

This, of course, has its own appeal, but it will not bear the light of God's revealed truth.

Can we ever really know then? Is it really the case that your guess is as good as mine? Must we settle for the compromise that you need to have your ideas and I mine?

In the end are we not all in the dark? Is there a reliable source of dependable information?

Science cannot help us here. It has many helpful and practical conclusions to give us about this life, but not about the next. Science by its very definition only deals with this world. It depends upon empirically verifiable facts – those things which can be tested by what we see, touch, hear, smell and taste.

Sentiment is equally unreliable in this sphere. Often sentiment is powerfully present within this context, but that does not give it legitimate authority. Indeed sentiment can be a most dangerous guide in considering the vast geography of life after death. Sentiment begins its creed with: 'I like to feel that . . .'.

Scripture alone can give us confidence. This is our only real source of knowledge. God has not left us in the dark. He has not told us all – but enough to enable us to prepare properly for the event. The Bible says very straightforward and demanding things about death.

1. *Death is real*

The Bible, as with life, takes death seriously and faces up to its reality. Indeed, an instrument of death lies at the heart of, and is a symbol for, the Christian faith – a Cross. Christianity declares that God himself faced death, as we know and understand it, in its most violent and degrading form because of the nature of sin.

2. *Death is an enemy*

The Scriptures are uncompromising here. Death is declared to be an intrusion into God's creation. It belongs to Satan's order not God's – and need never have happened to men and women. Sometimes death appears as a welcome alternative to what has become an intolerable and insupportable life – yet it remains as an enemy to be contested. To speak of it with warmth and in endearing terms is to be in conflict with the Bible.

3. Death is never the end for anyone

Jesus quite categorically said that 'all who are in the graves shall come forth' – there are no exemptions made! There may well be the separation of body and spirit at death (and there is!) but that is never the end of either body or spirit. This is what makes suicide not only tragically sad, but manifestly senseless.

4. Beyond death there is not one destiny but two

This is the clear teaching of the Bible – we are not all going to the same place, but to one of two places which we shall explore later. The life that we live now will prove decisive in guaranteeing which of these two destinies will be ours. What we do here before death will certainly determine what we shall be doing after death.

Death will be followed by judgment – not immediately, but assuredly there will be a day of reckoning and accountability. When all is said and done, it is this that makes death such an awesome event of life.

5. Death is a defeated enemy

The real problem in death lies in the reality of sin in man. But the Easter Gospel sweeps away the instinctive horror in the soul of man towards death. When Jesus died, was buried, and rose again death became a conquered foe because sin had been dealt with.

For this reason Jesus used a euphemism for death when He spoke of it. He speaks of those who have died as having 'fallen asleep'. We speak similarly of death with softer phrases. Sometimes, however, our verbal softening of death can be misleading. One of the frequent phrases we use is that the deceased has 'passed away'. Biblically this means 'utterly destroyed' and 'absolutely finished'. The Bible speaks of the world 'passing away' or prophecy 'passing away'. The implication is that neither will return – ever!! But when Jesus speaks of those who have died as having 'fallen asleep' He is speaking of a condition from which they can be roused and wakened. 'Good-night' will be followed by 'Good-morning'.

Because of this the Christian can look at death without pretending and fear can be substantially replaced by faith. Winston Churchill spoke of the death of King George VI in this way:

> During the last few months the King has walked with death as if it were a companion, an acquaintance whom he recognised and did not fear. During the last few months the King has been sustained, not only by his natural buoyancy of spirit, but by the sincerity of his Christian faith.

I can well remember the morning of that event. I was up at University and shortly after the King's death had been announced I attended a lecture given by the Professor of the Scottish History Department, Professor Mackie. He came in front of his class obviously upset and deeply moved. This elderly, avuncular figure spoke warmly of the late King's virtues, and before gathering his academic gown around him and retreating to his side room, with his cheeks wet with tears, he summed up his appraisal of the King: 'He lived as a Christian gentleman, and died with the assurance of Christian faith'.

In my own Christian agnosticism at that time, I felt a new shaft of light had broken through into my bewildered soul.

3: Death – Where is he now?

I remember going into a shattered, grief-stricken home one day to which sudden and totally unexpected death had come. It was evening and John had come home from work at the usual time and had complained that he felt unwell. Rather than clean up, sit down, and have his supper, he went straight upstairs to lie down. This was so unusual, that having done one or two things in the kitchen, Barbara went up to check that he was all right, and discovered that he had died.

As she looked at this tall, well-formed, hard-working, good man of hers there was only one question in her mind – 'Where is he now?' There was no panic, or hysteria, only that one demanding question – 'Where is he now?' There was neither recall of the past nor fear of the future at this stage, only that insistent question – 'Where is he now?' Her eyes told her – he is here, lying so still, so quiet, so peaceful! Her mind and heart told her – wherever he is, he is not here; that familiar frame is not him!

The ancient Greeks were puzzled by this very phenomenon. They were so disturbed by it that they weighed a person before he died and then afterwards and discovered that he weighed exactly the same on both occasions. Substantially he was the same, but manifestly he was quite different. Something clearly had gone! 'Where is he now?'

There is a lot of vagueness and uncertainty here, and often the language we use belies our confusion. Maybe the event of death makes it difficult for us to think clearly. Maybe the demand for life after death makes us more romantic than real. Maybe we have never sufficiently prepared for the event of death and so never really faced up to the facts of life after death. Who knows what causes our reluctance to answer that very simple and straightforward question: 'Where is he now?'

To be realistic, we need to ask a much more fundamental question: 'What is man?' When we speak of a man or a woman, what are we really talking about? There are two self-evident parts to man's nature:

1. *He comprises what is seen and natural – his body*

This part of a man can be scrutinised. The behaviour of his body with its actions and reactions; its functions and malfunctions can be monitored. Its constituent parts can be examined and a verdict passed on them – they are either normal or abnormal. It is on this part of him that man normally spends most of his time and money. He feeds it; washes it; clothes it; exercises it; rests it; perfumes it; decorates it; disciplines it; indulges it; protects it. Undoubtedly to man his body is important. The scientist's analysis of his body would cause him to regard it as a joke. The scientist concludes that the average man has enough fat to make seven bars of soap; enough iron to make a medium-sized nail; enough sugar to fill a sugar-sifter; enough lime to white-wash a hen house; enough potassium to explode a toy cannon; enough magnesium for a dose of magnesia; enough phosphorus to make the tips of 2,200 matches – and a little sulphur. In the early Thirties, Harry Emerson Fosdick, a well-known Baptist minister in New York, commented on this sardonically: 'You could buy the lot for two dollars'. Whatever the exchange rate, either then or now, it does not amount to very much. The anatomist, and the pathologist, and indeed others would have to rate man's body, however, rather higher in terms of its functioning.

So far as Christians are concerned the body is very important. After all Jesus took upon Himself a human body. This was the means which God used to express Himself: 'For God was pleased to have all His fullness dwell in Him . . .' Presumably this is the ultimate mystery – that God came to earth in a human body. It was this which filled Wesley with wonder and awe, and so he sang:

Our God contracted to a span
Incomprehensibly made man.

A writer tells how in Deeside in Scotland there is on the mantelpiece of a certain house a cracked and chipped common kitchen cup. The cup is actually under a glass case and no one is allowed to handle it except with the greatest care. How did that cup get there? Once, many years ago, a carriage drove up to a Deeside cottage. The coachman got down and went to the door and said that his passenger was thirsty. Could she please have a drink of water? The lady in the cottage did not want to risk one of her good cups, so she took an old chipped kitchen cup, filled it at the tap, and took it out. The lady in the carriage thanked her, took the cup and drank and the coachman drove away. Now the lady in that cottage was a newcomer to the district; and no sooner had the coach driven away than her neighbours were at her door. 'What did she say to you?' was demanded. 'You were fortunate indeed to get a visit like that!' they said. The lady of the cottage said, 'What on earth are you talking about? I have just given a drink to a lady who was thirsty. That's all.' 'But', they said, 'don't you know who that lady was?' 'I haven't an idea', the lady of the cottage said. Then the others told her, 'That was Queen Victoria'. The Queen was staying at Balmoral Castle as she often did. The lady of the cottage was overwhelmed. To think that she had chosen her oldest kitchen cup out of which to give her Queen a drink! At first she was so ashamed she did not know what to do; but then she took the cup and put it under a glass cover and the cup became her most cherished possession and no one else was allowed to use it, and it became a family heirloom because it had been touched by the hands and lips of the Queen. A common kitchen cup had become a thing of value because the Queen had touched it.

Forever our bodies must be so regarded. With all their

inadequacy and imperfection this was the means that God used to show us what He is like.

Added to this is the Christian awareness that it is through our bodies that God still wants to manifest the character and conduct of Christ through the fruit and gifts of the Holy Spirit. I was brought up to believe that the Church building was the house of God. That had some very significant practical implications. The building was revered for its own sake. But although the Old Testament teaches that God dwells in buildings, the New Testament clearly indicates that God dwells in people by the power of His Holy Spirit. We, as Christians together, are the Body of Christ on earth. Jesus is in heaven now in His 'human' body since His Ascension. So God requires a new Body on earth through which He can manifest His life – so through our birth and baptism in the Holy Spirit we have become just that.

It was because of this that God said: 'Let there be . . .' for the rest of creation, but for man He said: 'Let us make . . .'. Our bodies are not simply awesome in their performance, but also in their purpose.

It is pagan philosophy and practice which either indulges or despises the human body – the Christian delights in it as a previous gift from God and so looks after it with a godly discipline. Through the centuries every Christian creed has proclaimed its belief in the resurrection of the body. As we shall notice together there is only a temporary separation between the unseen part of man and the seen part of man (his body) at death. There is a day coming when spirit and body will come together again. Had the ancient Greeks stood to recite their creed, they would have said: 'I believe in the immortality of the soul'. They believed that the soul was imprisoned in the body, but at death release came as the prison house was now destroyed and so the spiritual part could go on for ever.

What happens to the body when a person dies? Quite clearly certain physical processes stop immediately –

breathing, circulation, heart-beat, etc. Other physical processes, however, seem to continue for a very short time – for example the hair continues to grow. After a time these stop too, and disintegration and decomposition become rapid.

2. He comprises what is unseen and supernatural – his soul and his spirit

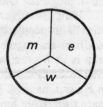

The *soul* of man comprises his *mind* (*m*); his *emotions* (*e*) and his *will* (*w*). None of these aspects of him is visible although undoubtedly real. But man has another invisible part to his nature which is just as real – his *spirit*. It is this part that God the Holy Spirit wants to invade at the time of his Christian conversion. So man might be shown in a diagram as follows:

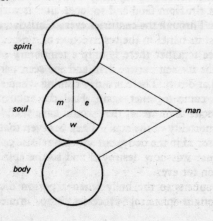

The Bible is emphatic that man is more than a body. If he is only a concoction of chemicals and glands, enzymes and hormones; and a quite remarkable engineering feat, then it is easy to answer the question: 'What happens immediately when I die?'. This remarkable phenomenon ceases to function and begins to disintegrate! The Bible, however, speaks of the human body as a tent or a dwelling place. The apostle Paul speaks confidently of the day when he will no longer live in his tent. Others have expressed themselves in a similar way.

Dr Guthrie confides: 'They say I am growing old because my hair is silvered, and there are crow's-feet on my forehead, and my step is not as firm and elastic as before. But they are mistaken; that is not me. The knees are weak, but the knees are not me. The brow is wrinkled, but the brow is not me. This is the house I live in, but I am young, younger than I was ever before.'

Once someone asked John Quincey Adams how he was, and he replied: 'Thank you, John Quincey Adams is very well in himself, sir; but the house in which he lives is falling to pieces. Time and seasons have nearly destroyed it. The roof is well worn, the walls shattered. It trembles with every gale. I think John Quincey Adams will soon have to move out. But he himself is very well, sir.'

So people have expressed themselves as they have faced up to the reality that there is another aspect to them which is not seen and natural. The seen and the unseen; the natural and the supernatural; are intimately connected and closely linked together. In fact our human experience has never known them apart, and so we cannot conceive the reality of such a thing. At death, however, this is precisely what happens – the seen and natural is separated from the unseen and the supernatural. However the doctor may determine and describe death, this in fact, is what we really mean when we say: 'He is dead!' We, of course, recognise this in popular speech: 'Don't give up the ghost yet!' 'I need to keep body and soul together!' 'S.O.S. – save our souls!' –

keep our souls in our bodies!; keep us alive!; keep us from death!

In that dramatic moment when Jesus had completed so perfectly the task God had given Him to do, He cried out in a loud voice: 'Father, into your hands I commit My spirit!' – notice not 'Myself' nor 'My body', but 'My spirit'. In his gospel Luke (and he was a doctor) adds: 'When He had said this He breathed His last.'

His mother He entrusted to John; His clothes were taken by the soldiers; His body was looked after lovingly by His friends; but His spirit was committed to His Father. Those who believe in life after death see that whatever else it includes at death such life does not include the body. The body must be left behind at that moment when we leave the land of the dying and enter the land of the living.

Let me hasten to add, however, that Christians believe 'in the resurrection of the body and the life everlasting'. At some future point that which has been separated at death comes together again and the seen and the unseen are re-united. The corruptible will become incorruptible, and what in this world has been a bridgehead for sin becomes a bridgehead for glory in the next. However strange and incredible this may seem we confidently believe it to be so for two undeniable reasons. First of all, Jesus did unite the seen and the unseen for a few people during His earthly life. Each was in a different phase of disintegration. The little daughter of Jairus had just died; the son of the widow who lived in Nain was about to be buried; Jesus' dear friend Lazarus, in whose home He had known such loving and tender hospitality, had already been buried and his body had been decomposing for four days. It is true that He brought them back to *this* life and not to the *next* so that they would go through the experience of death yet again. However, it did indicate that He had the power to unite the seen and the unseen.

Secondly, Jesus experienced this re-uniting of the seen and the unseen in the event which we call Easter. This occurred three days after He committed His spirit to His Father and three days after His body had been tenderly, though hurriedly, committed to the tomb. This is the very heart of the Christian Gospel. Many Christians have not yet fully come to terms with it, but that does not deny its reality. The resurrection of Jesus Christ stands as the ultimate challenge to the world as the incarnation of Jesus Christ stands as the ultimate mystery. Significantly, before His death Jesus drew attention to the spiritual (unseen) aspects of His nature, whilst after His resurrection He continually drew attention to the physical (seen) aspects of His nature. When He came back from the dead in resurrection He insisted He was not a disembodied spirit any longer and demanded that His disciples who had known Him so well would authenticate that—'Touch Me! See for yourselves! Prove it to your own satisfaction! A spirit does not have flesh and bones nor can it enjoy your breakfast!'

This, of course, is the major difference between Christian and non-Christian belief in life after death. Some non-Christians would subscribe to the fact that we survive the event which we call death—but only as disembodied spirits. Christians, on the other hand, declare unequivocally that a day is coming when we will live again as embodied spirits. We believe in the resurrection in the body. We believe in the redemption of the body—for which we all eagerly wait. We believe that when God 'saves' a person, He does not just save his spirit and his soul (the unseen and the supernatural), but one day He will save his body (the seen and the natural) too, so that we may at last become what He always intended us to be.

We are now in a more intelligent position to answer the original question: 'Where is he now?' From reading the Gospels there is a clear indication that for Jesus there was an *interval* between death and resurrection—between the separating of the seen and the unseen, and their re-uniting. So it is with us! For Jesus it was a comparatively short experience; for us it may well be considerably longer. Length of time, however, is not the issue which concerns us here. The fact of the matter is that there is a period when the seen and the unseen are apart.

There are many other questions which are much more relevant than 'How long does this last?' We are much more concerned to know, 'What will it be like?' 'What will happen to us during that time?' 'Will we be unconscious or awake?' 'Where, in fact, will we be?' 'What will we be doing?' For Jesus it only lasted three days and three nights — but Christians have always been aware that it would be a mistake to say that He was in heaven. The Apostles' Creed encapsulates it most straightforwardly when it says, almost tersely: 'He descended into Hades'. Perhaps the verb 'descended' has misled us. Perhaps the noun 'Hades' has not been properly understood. The English alteration to 'Hell' is certainly inaccurate and so unfortunate. Hades does not equal Hell. In fact Hades is not necessarily a bad word or a bad place. It simply means 'the realm or place of the departed spirits'. Whatever the departed spirits are doing, or wherever the departed spirits are — the New Testament says they are in Hades (Greek) whilst the Old Testament says they are in Sheol (Hebrew). The Old Testament has little to say about Hell, but a great deal about Sheol or Hades. What is really being said is that there is an interval — a state in between — between death and resurrection. The Apostles' Creed again makes a very clear statement about Jesus when it says: 'The third day He rose again from the dead. He ascended into heaven.' Heaven and Hell are kept for the person who has been resurrected bodily. It would be so much more helpful, accurate and consistent if Christians kept the word Heaven for *after* the resurrection when we shall have bodies and live in the place which is being prepared for us now.

For the Christian Hades (Sheol) is described by Jesus as *paradise*. To most of us this word in its Biblical context — *paradise* — is used by Jesus to give assurance to one of His companions who was with Him on Calvary on that first Good Friday. Jesus was crucified between two criminals. One taunted Him, whilst for the other there was an awakening to the fact of who Jesus was in the last hours of his life. It began to dawn upon him that Jesus was who He claimed to be – the Messiah; the Christ; the Son of God. Even in death Jesus' authority and dignity was not dimmed. Believing Jesus to be the Messiah, and thinking of some distant day in the future, he cried out before he was no longer able to do so: 'Jesus, remember me when You come into Your Kingdom'. He was concerned that Jesus would not forget him at the end of history. However, Jesus said: 'I will do more for you, and better for you, than that! I will do something for you *today*! *Now*! Today you will be with Me in *paradise*!' Jesus does not use the word *heaven* here – and He is always careful in His use of words. He deliberately uses this word *paradise* so we can comfort Christians, not with some distant destination, but with this present reality – *paradise*.

Paradise is a particularly beautiful word. It is a Persian word and means 'an exquisite garden'. It refers particularly to a royal garden – a garden which belongs to the King or the Queen. It would be used for the garden of Buckingham Palace in London – for example. This latter is not open to the public. In fact it is guarded to ensure that no one intrudes into it, and is hidden by and large from public view. The Queen can enjoy that garden any time she wishes; we can only enjoy it by her express invitation. We never simply happen to be there – we can only go in if we are officially invited by name by the Queen. *Paradise* is also used of the Garden of Eden – the location described in the earliest part of the Bible and now identified as being in the land of Armenia, where the River Tigris and the River Euphrates meet – one from the Black Sea and the other from the Caspian Sea. This is not fantasy, but fact. Again, *paradise* is used at the end of the Bible for the Garden City.

It is important to notice that the Garden and the Palace

are different. When Jesus speaks of His Father's House, He is not referring to His Father's Garden, but rather to the final destination of those who have been born into His Father's family. On the eve of His death Jesus comforted His anxious disciples by telling them: 'In My Father's House are many rooms; if it were not so I would have told you. I am going there to prepare a place for you. And if I go and prepare a place for you, I will come back and take you to be with Me, that you also may be where I am.' Jesus said to the criminal who shared His death throes on that frightful Good Friday afternoon: 'Although I cannot take you now to My Father's House, I can take you to the King's Garden. We will be there together you and I. We will not be separated after death.'

London has always held a great fascination for me. Even now after having lived many years just outside it, London still fills me with a sense of wonder. I suppose subconsciously I am aware of its aura of history – so much has happened there! I suppose I still feel the tingle in my spine that used to come when, as a boy, I heard Alvar Liddell or John Snagge give a news bulletin during the war. The first stroke of Big Ben was always followed by three words which to me spelled magnificence and dispelled any hesitancy or uncertainty: 'This is London'. It was in this atmosphere that I heard some of the stirring broadcasts of Winston Churchill and on a quite different note the late King George VI. The London Bobby and the red London bus are both part of the scene. Occasionally I have ridden on one of these London buses and it is possible to ride alongside Buckingham Palace. It is quite impossible to see into the Palace itself, but you can catch glimpses of the garden – where distinguished and undistinguished guests are invited from time to time. I found this concept helpful when thinking of life after death.

Stage one is the life we now live here. It is rather like being on the top deck of a London bus. You are aware that the Palace and the garden are there. The inside of the Palace is hidden from public view, but from the vantage point of a 'double-decker' you can catch a glimpse of the garden.

Stage two is the interval between death and resurrection. It would be equated with receiving a personal invitation from the Queen to join her in her garden for a Royal Garden Party – to be with her and her family and the other invited guests. Now it would not be something viewed imperfectly from afar, but the opportunity has now been given to see it personally and enjoy it fully in the company of others.

Stage three is the final resurrection which is timed to be an accompaniment of the triumphant return of our Lord Jesus. Then, if you will, we are not simply invited into the garden, but into the Palace, and we are shown to our special apartments which are prepared and reserved for us.

Paradise, then, is very much better than anything we have known in this life. We shall have the unimaginable joy of being with the King in His Garden and enjoying the fellowship of all who have responded to His personal invitation. Here is the direct answer to those who ask: 'Are we awake or asleep; aware or unaware; conscious or unconscious?'

There are those who believe in soul sleep. They are found mainly among the cults, although I do remember a dear Christian man who was wholly persuaded of this and did his best to convince me too by letter, conversation, and little booklet. He has since gone to be with the Lord and I sometimes wonder how he is getting on. The New Testament does indeed speak of the dead as being 'asleep'. But sleep is a physical function – the soul and the spirit do not sleep; only bodies can sleep. When the Bible speaks of those who die as having 'fallen asleep' it is referring to the appearance of the body. Of course to say someone has fallen asleep is to assume that it is possible to rouse and waken up that person.

With characteristic enthusiasm, and expressing the wonder of his heart, the Apostle Paul says: 'He died for us so that, whether we are awake or asleep, we may live together with Him.' That is the glorious thing – we are to be with Christ! As I can be aware of Him in this life, so in the next – only more so! How else could it be when again that dynamic, purposeful human being Paul, poured out his heart to the Christians from Philippi who had been so thoughtful and generous towards him: 'If I am to go on living in the body, this will mean fruitful labour for me. Yet what shall I choose? I do not know! I am torn between the two: I desire to depart and be with Christ, which is better by far; but it is more necessary for you that I remain in the body.' Were it only himself to please there is no doubt in his mind, but there were other considerations to be faced with honesty and with honour. For him – as for us – there was the prospect of enjoying the company of Christ: '. . . we are always confident and know that as long as we are at home in the body we are away from the Lord. We live by faith, not by sight. We are confident, I say, and would prefer to be away from the body and at home with the Lord.' He is saying quite clearly that he would rather be disembodied and so enjoy unhindered fellowship with Jesus. This is the yearning of his heart if there were no other considerations to be taken into account. But there is more – not only conscious fellowship with Christ, but also a similar experience with those who are the servants of God. After all Jesus speaks about Lazarus finding himself being taken by the angels to be next to Abraham in the garden. He may have longed to eat the crumbs that fell from the bread with which the guests of the rich man cleaned their hands as they ate at his table, and could not, but now God had made sure that it was not just crumbs he enjoyed, but the company of the 'father of the faithful'. As we shall see, too, the Palace Staff are waiting to serve us in the garden – the angels will be there. Even if we die alone – God has His angels waiting to take care of us. We may well dismiss angels to the realm of fantasy, and consider them as we consider fairies or Santa Claus. We may never even consider them apart from Christmas carols and nativity plays – but after we die we will believe in them, for they will be there, not now just to do God's bidding but ours too!

But what of the unrepentant dead? What of those who gave no place to God in this life – not always bad people, but often people of good intention and generous heart? Sentiment would demand it otherwise, as we have already noted, but there are strong indications in the Bible that the *interval* between death and resurrection is located not only in a garden *paradise*, but also in a *prison*. In this life many palaces have not only a garden which the king enjoys and invites others to enjoy, but they also have a prison – a dungeon. One of the most extraordinary verses in the Bible occurs in that fascinating first letter which Peter wrote to Christians who were having to live under intense pressure. He writes in this way: 'For Christ died for sins once for all, the righteous for the unrighteous, to bring you to God. He was put to death in the body, but made alive in the Spirit, through whom also He went and preached to the spirits in prison who disobeyed long ago . . .'

So there is another place to which we could go immediately after death – *prison* not *paradise*! Although heaven and hell are not our immediate destination there will be a clear distinction between those who die 'in faith' and those who do not. One destination is likened to a Garden whilst the other is described as a Prison – and both belong to God.

It would seem that this latter is characterised by two disturbing features. It is *first of all* a place of *segregation* – from God and God's people. Judas will be there – since we are told that, having betrayed Christ and hanged himself, he went to 'his own place'. Some of the angels will be there, since we learn from the Bible that one-third of the angels created by God rebelled against Him and desired to take over His Kingdom. Twice in the New Testament we are told that God has put some of these in custody until the time of their final trial. The other criminal who was executed at the same time as Jesus – he will be there!

This *prison* then will not involve solitary confinement. There will be many there! These will be those who were content to live apart from God and God's people in this life – God will not infringe that desire in the next life! It could be, of course, that it will only be then that they realise how much they really do miss God and His people.

Secondly it will be a place of *suffering*. It would appear from the little which we do know about it that memory will be active, and so there will be conscious regret that life is over and death has sealed the decisions taken there – whether conscious or careless. Regret will also be experienced that the future course is unalterably set and no change can now be made.

Two things are quite certain from what we know. *One* is that you cannot go back to life on earth from that prison. *Two* is that you cannot go forward to the Garden of God from that prison. Perhaps the most devastating thing of all about prison is that freedom is now restricted.

I can remember going across from Dunfermline to Edinburgh's Saughton Prison to meet a prisoner, who had served his sentence, and bring him home. I had visited him there regularly as he worked out his sentence. It was the early Spring and when I left home in my car it was still dark. In those days there was no Forth Road Bridge to enable easy access to Edinburgh from the North. The crossing was made on a chain-driven car ferry. Crossing the River Forth at the best of times can be a very cold experience – the wind often develops a whip-like quality. On that morning it was bitterly cold. I arrived early at the prison and waited for that moving moment when the doors are opened and prisoners are released. One is aware of their uncertainty and almost embarrassment. On that particular morning there were only a few prisoners discharged and even fewer were there to greet them. I greeted my friend and then we travelled back to Dunfermline together in my car. We arrived at South Queensferry and boarded the ferry for the short trip across the River Forth. Despite the biting wind, he insisted on getting out of the car and going up on the 'deck' of the ferry. Day had come fully, but the temperature had not improved. However, physical discomfort had little restraint when it came to realising the sweet smell of freedom. He returned to the warm car windswept and red-nosed, but deeply gratified by the experience.

However, there is no such experience of freedom in the prison involved in the life which follows this life – ever! Disembodied spirits do not require a *place* to dwell as we know it. It requires the resurrection and the re-uniting of body and spirit for such a place to be needed. That will come, but in the meantime we need not think of *paradise* and *prison* as places as we would understand that concept. That must not bring us to a conclusion that they have no reality in fact. After all, God has described our future in two main words – indescribable and unimaginable!

4: Death – But not the end

Some years ago on television David Frost hosted a programme on the theme of death. Well-known personalities were asked to state their views. In spite of the inconclusiveness and unsatisfactoriness of the programme two things emerged that we have noticed already. First of all there was uncertainty and confusion among otherwise intelligent people about death. 'I think that possibly, perhaps, or maybe . . .' There was a lot of guesswork! Secondly, fear had quite clearly established itself in each mind for one reason or another. Someone said, during the course of the programme, that 'the fear of death is so natural that all life is one long effort not to think about it'.

This is why death is a no-go area today – the vast majority of people are afraid to die. It is possible to discuss death and even to argue about it, but inescapably we have to face its reality at some point and so we run away from it for as long as possible. George Bernard Shaw impresses its reality upon us in his own inimitable way when he says: 'Death is the ultimate statistic: one out of one dies.'

Apart from the Christian Faith there really are no real answers in the face of death. Bertrand Russell, for example, gives no hope for the future, only despair; no comfort to the aching heart like Tennyson's who longed for 'the touch of a vanished hand and the sound of a voice that is still'; no security of knowing there is a place being prepared for us; no sense of justice that at last right will be established over wrong. He expresses the ultimate horror of atheism in his book *Why I Am Not A Christian*:

When I die I shall rot, and nothing of my ego shall survive . . . There is darkness without and when I die there will be darkness within. There is no splendour, no vastness anywhere; only triviality for a moment, and then nothing.

David Watson records how a young person expressed that same awfulness of 'and then nothing':

I lie awake worrying what it will be like to be dead,
I lie awake worrying how dark will the coffin be.
I lie awake and feel how cold my life will be.
It makes no sense the end of life being death.
Just a memory, and then nothing,
Absolutely nothing, just nothing.
Death is like a black hole without any sides.
Death is like a thought without a thinker.
Death is fear . . .

Long ago the ancient Greeks, who thought so deeply, hardly gave much more encouragement. They certainly recognised that man is much more than a body. They appreciated that he is a soul too and concluded that at death the soul is released from the body. They regarded the body as the prison house of the soul, and so at death the soul was released from its prison to go on eternally free, but disembodied. This lies at the heart of a great deal of pagan philosophy on death. The more popular belief in re-incarnation which has an increasing appeal in the Western world today contributes little more to enable us to face death without fear. Those who hold this view believe that the unseen part of us will return to inhabit someone else's body – or even in another body on earth. We will be re-born again and again on this very same earth until finally we lose our identity by being absorbed into some kind of universal consciousness.

The Christian Faith has declared in every generation, with a very demanding confidence, that whilst at death body and spirit are undoubtedly separated, the day will come when body and spirit will be re-united. Perhaps its very confidence causes a strong reaction. Even in Jesus' day there was a faction amongst the Jews called the Sadducees. They were the liberal wing of Judaism – as the Pharisees were the conservative wing. They could not accept the reality of the supernatural. The main areas of their antagonism with the Pharisees lay there. The re-uniting of spirit and body in resurrection; the reality of angels and spirits were all anathema to them. So there was division even in religious life over the resurrection of the body. Among the intellectuals of Jesus' day, there was an equally strong antipathy. Luke tells us that the Greeks listened to Paul teaching on God, judgment, human life and conscience with interest. But then he used a word which made them laugh – 'resurrection'. 'When they heard about the resurrection of the dead, some of them sneered, but others said, "We want to hear you again on this subject." '

In the twentieth century the voices of science and technology have said in a number of ways: 'If Christianity is to survive in the modern world then the idea of resurrection will need to be discarded.' Their objection is two-fold. First of all it is too *materialistic*. It makes heaven a place and the after-life too like this one. However, it is the Bible which encourages us to think in this way. While there are mysteries and the terminology which is used is difficult for us to grasp, nevertheless there are indications that our experience here is a shadow of the substance which we will experience there. However difficult it may be for us to conceive, this is what Jesus said and this is what the Bible indicates. Only our proud minds – which have such serious limitations – would cause us to doubt what God has revealed. The second objection to the idea of resurrection is that it is too *miraculous*. A miracle is a natural event in that it occurs within the context of nature; which follows an unnatural course in that it cuts across the normal pattern of nature; and has a supernatural cause or origin in that it depends upon God and not man. By this definition resurrection from the dead is surely a miracle – perhaps the miracle of miracles! It is beyond man's ability to grasp and man's power to do – and so it becomes suspect to him! How could God gather together the cells of a person totally decomposed or disintegrated through burial, cremation or accident and so achieve resurrection of the body? The question, of course, is absurd apart from the reality of God. We are so prone to limit God to our own concepts and achievements – God can only do what is within the limits of the conceivable and the possible for me. By and large there has been a dividing of the supernatural from the heart of the Christianity of the Western world. One of the thrilling things which is happening again, however, is that God is teaching us slowly and patiently that He has called us as Christians to be naturally supernatural and supernaturally natural.

Where is the ground of our certainty? Can we be sure that though death is so real, it is not the end? Can we know that we will have a new body some day? Or is it the case that many are right when they feel in the midst of all the facts and the uncertainties that my guess is as good as yours? There is one fact which when examined historically and even scientifically according to any honourable laws of examination of the past stands out like some factual Rock of Gibraltar – *the resurrection of Jesus Christ.*

That Jesus Christ was a real, historical person would hardly be doubted today. Dr F. F. Bruce, formerly Rylands Professor of Biblical Criticism and Exegesis at the University of Manchester has rightly said:

> Some writers may toy with the fancy of a 'Christ-myth',
> but they do not do so on the ground of historical
> evidence. The historicity of Christ is as axiomatic for
> an unbiased historian as the historicity of Julius Caesar.
> It is not historians who propagate the 'Christ-myth'
> theories.

Non-Christian historians would substantiate Bruce's conclusion that Jesus Christ of Nazareth was undoubtedly a figure in history. For example, the Roman historian, Tacitus, who was the son-in-law of Julius Agricola, the Governor of Britain in AD 80–84, affirms this. While writing of the reign of Nero, he alludes to the death of Christ and to the existence of Christians in Rome:

> But not all the relief that could come from man, nor all the bounties that the prince could bestow, nor all the atonements which could be presented to the gods, availed to relieve Nero from the infamy of being believed to have ordered the conflagration, the fire of Rome. Hence to suppress the rumour, he falsely charged with the guilt, and punished with the most exquisite tortures, the persons commonly called Christians, who were hated for their enormities. Christus, the founder of the name, was put to death by Pontius Pilate, procurator of Judea in the reign of Tiberius: but the pernicious superstition, repressed for a time broke out again, not only through Judea, where the mischief originated, but through the city of Rome also.

Significantly the *Encyclopaedia Britannica*, in one of its most recent editions, used 20,000 words in describing this person, Jesus. His description takes more space than is given to Aristotle, Cicero, Alexander, Julius Caesar, Buddha, Confucius, Mohammed or Napoleon Bonaparte.

Christianity not only declares the *reality* of Christ, but also, with equal clarity and conviction, the *resurrection* of Christ. In his book *Man Alive* Michael Green, Rector of St Aldate's, Oxford makes the point well:

> Christianity does not hold the resurrection to be one among many tenets of belief. Without faith in the resurrection there would be no Christianity at all. The

Christian Church would never have begun; the Jesus-movement would have fizzled out like a damp squib with his execution. Christianity stands or falls with the truth of the resurrection. Once disprove it, and you have disposed of Christianity. Christianity is a historical religion. It claims that God has taken the risk of involving himself in human history, and the facts are there for you to examine with the utmost rigour. They will stand any amount of critical investigation.

For me Easter morning among many, many memorable occasions throughout the year is the most moving of all. For many years now we have met at 7.30 am for Communion. We share Communion often, but there is something quite unique about that morning. The whole atmosphere is pervaded by an excitement, an expectancy, an anticipation, a sense of wonder. I know that this is a very subjective thing, but nevertheless it is undeniably real. Communion over, there is the warm greeting of one another in a traditional Easter way. The other Christian festivals are filled with joy and reality, but none quite like this one. We share breakfast together in a crowded hall. It is a good breakfast – beautifully prepared and lovingly served – but there is something extra on that morning which neither food nor fellowship can provide. Breakfast over, the Christian family begins to gather in the main part of the building for worship. Even as I write about it now I can sense the anticipation and the joy that wells up from that crowded congregation. As I give the Easter greeting: 'Christ is risen!' there is laughter and sparkling eyes as the traditional reply is given: 'He is risen indeed!'

Never was that greeting more movingly given in Czechoslovakia than when a Russian lecturer was addressing a packed audience on the subject of resurrection from the standpoint of atheistic Communism. Speaking at considerable length he roundly discredited it to the level of folklore and fairy-tale. The Czechoslovakian theologian who tells the story relates how an Orthodox priest asked the lecturer if he might reply. He was warned that he would only be given five minutes to do so. 'Five minutes?', he exclaimed, 'five seconds is all I need!' He turned to the audience and gave the Easter greeting characteristic of the Eastern Orthodox Church – 'Christos aneste!' – 'Christ is risen!' Back from the vast concourse of people came the deafening roar of the traditional reply, 'Alethos aneste!' – 'Truly, He is risen!' No amount of argument and debate can stifle the living reality of personal experience!

Such an important issue however demands a much firmer base than that which is built by personal subjective experience. The fact that I want it to be true more than anything else is no guarantee that it is so. Are there objective, verifiable grounds for such a dramatic and revolutionising reality? Yes, indeed there are! In fact there is evidence which is as good as, if not better than, the evidence for most if not for all the events of history recorded 2,000 years ago. What is this evidence?

1. The birth and growth of the Christian Church

The disciples of Jesus were not disposed to believe that He had risen and conquered death. In fact on that appalling first Good Friday they were despondent and despairing. In spite of all the Lord had said the grim reality which confronted their eyes put paid to any nascent hope that what He had promised could ever in fact be true – Jesus was finished and faith destroyed. Any talk of resurrection was regarded as fairy tale and wishful thinking – nothing could touch their gloom and heartbreak. However, historical and psychological miracle that it is, these depressed and disillusioned disciples were filled with such a joyous conviction that Jesus had risen from the dead that they were prepared to realise His other great promise to them – that the Holy Spirit would come upon them in power and enabling – and so they were able to go out and turn the world upside-down or put the world at last right way up.

Through dark days and deep waters the Church has come through the years until these exciting days in which we are now living. Today the Church is growing faster than at any other time in her history. The historian Kenneth Scott Latourette makes the confident conclusion that:

It was the conviction of the resurrection of Jesus which lifted His followers out of the despair into which His death had cast them and which led to the perpetuation of the movement begun by Him. But for their profound belief that the crucified had risen from the dead and that they had seen Him and talked with Him, the death of Jesus and even Jesus Himself would probably have been all but forgotten.

These indeed are exciting days in which to be alive and to be part of the living Body of Jesus Christ on earth – the Church. To share in what Jesus promised so many years ago and to experience the pulsing of His life flowing through ordinary people and so fulfilling His purposes is an indescribable joy. That deadness is being transformed by life, and formality changed by faith, cannot be doubted – even here in the West! 'Truly, Christ is risen!'

2. *The existence of the New Testament*
It takes little understanding to realise that the New Testament could never have been written apart from the resurrection of Christ. There is a uniting, undergirding conviction in all those who were responsible for writing the New Testament that Jesus did not remain dead, but defeated it and is alive. The New Testament was written at least twenty years *after* the event of Calvary – during which time there was persecution which was considerable. In this climate any conviction of resurrection had time to waver and die. This, however, it did not do. Canon J. B. Phillips, who spent many years paraphrasing the Bible from the original documents and so challenging the climate of

antiquity which can so easily destroy its relevance to the twentieth century, says quite simply:

These (New Testament) Letters were written over quite a period of years, but there is not the slightest discernible diminution of faith. It was borne in upon me with irresistible force that these Letters could never have been written at all if there had been no Jesus Christ, no crucifixion, and no resurrection.

3. *The tomb where Jesus was buried was empty*

Whatever explanation may be given for it, the fact remains that where the body of Jesus had been laid in death was now empty. The message of a risen Christ could not have been maintained for a single moment in Jerusalem if the emptiness of the tomb and the disappearance of the body had not been established as plain fact.

The persuasive fact in all this is that neither friend nor enemy of Jesus could – or did – produce the body. The disciples could not, because His body was no longer on earth, but was now in heaven as a result of the Resurrection and the Ascension. They lived and were prepared to die because of their absolute assurance that it was so. Fantasy never transformed cowards into martyrs – and young martyrs at that! The Romans could not produce the body of Christ, even though they were embarrassed by an obvious breach of security and the Roman military machine was seen to be suspect. The penalty of death could not do anything to alter their confusion since the tomb had been sealed and guarded by the Roman authorities. The ultimate trump card of the Jewish authorities would have been to produce the bruised and beaten body of Christ. This would have silenced the preaching of a risen and reigning Christ forever which soon began to trouble the whole known world, reaching Rome itself within about thirty years.

There really is only one satisfactory conclusion to all this – that the tomb was empty because Christ was risen, and no one could give any other satisfactory, authenticated reason for the disappearance of the body, because there was none. George Hanson sums it up by saying:

> The simple faith of the Christian who believes in the Resurrection is nothing compared to the credulity of the sceptic who will accept the wildest and most improbable romances rather than admit the plain witness of historical certainties. The difficulties of belief may be great; the absurdities of unbelief are greater.

4. *The resurrection appearances of Jesus*

Jesus was seen over a period of six weeks on eleven different occasions by around five hundred and fifty people – sometimes in a group; sometimes alone. Many of these people were still alive when these 'evidences' were recorded. How can it be possible to dismiss all of this as mass hysteria or group dynamics or auto-suggestion?

In his excellent little book on the *Resurrection* Professor J. N. D. Anderson speaks very clearly on this issue:

> The most drastic way of dismissing the evidence would be to say that these stories were mere fabrications, that they were pure lies. But, so far as I know, not a single critic today would take such an attitude. In fact it really would be an impossible position. Think of the number of witnesses, over 500. Think of the character of the witnesses, men and women who gave the world the highest ethical teaching it has ever known, and who even on the testimony of their enemies lived it out in their lives. Think of the psychological absurdity of picturing a little band of defeated cowards cowering in an upper room one day and a few days later transformed into a company that no persecution could silence – and then attempting to attribute this dramatic change to nothing more convincing than a miserable

fabrication they were trying to foist upon the world. That simply wouldn't make sense.

5. *The reality of Christian testimony*

Literally millions of Christians have testified over a period of 2,000 years that they know Jesus is real and alive in their own experience. Some of these have come from other Faiths and their deep emotional involvement there is not readily convinced. Others have come from the background and conviction of a humanistic atheism and their claim to intellectual respectability is never easily challenged because of their fear of an irrational naïveté. Still others have come from a purely nominal faith where their religion was understood simply in terms of this life and any intrusion of the supernatural was shunned.

I received a letter from a young woman, whom I had first met as a sixth former, who was not disposed to believe – indeed, although a lovely person, she was rebellious in her heart and resisted any overtures to understand and embrace the Gospel of Christ. Judy had come to an evening service in our church and subsequently wrote the following:

A week later the Lord spoke to me. In fact He had been speaking to me for quite a time, but I hadn't wanted to obey. But this time He spoke so clearly I couldn't disobey any more. The result was that I got baptised in the Spirit.

I think, perhaps especially since that day the Lord has really come to mean so much more to me. He has given me so much and I don't have to qualify for any of His gifts because they are free. I've never known such love and peace and joy in my life before.

It's all so incredible. I've never felt so happy and joyous about anything before in my whole life. The Lord's given me such peace and I know that He is with me through all my problems. His love is so wonderful. It's becoming very precious to me and it's great to know He loves me whatever I do.

On another level altogether two young men went up to Oxford University many years ago. They were friends of Samuel Johnson and Alexander Pope. They were very much involved with the 'society group' of the day. Writing at the same time, Bishop Butler, the philosopher had concluded: 'It has come to be taken for granted that Christianity is not so much a subject for enquiry, but that it is now at length discovered to be fictitious.' It was against this background that these two able young men, Gilbert West and Lord Lyttleton, determined to attack the very basis of the Christian Faith. Lyttleton settled down to prove that Saul of Tarsus was never converted to Christ and West to demonstrate that Jesus never rose from the dead. Later they met to discuss their finds and discovered, a little sheepishly, that quite independently they had come to similar and disturbing conclusions.

Lyttleton found, on examination, that Saul of Tarsus did become a radically new man in Christ. West found that evidence pointed unmistakably to the fact that Jesus did rise from the dead. His book, which appeared subsequently, can still be found in a large library. It was published in 1747 and bears a title typical of the day – *Observation on the History and Evidences of the Resurrection of Jesus Christ*.

On the flyleaf is a very significant quotation from Ecclesiasticus 11:7 which might be adopted with profit by any modern agnostic and is a summary of West's own testimony, 'Blame not before thou hast examined the truth'.

Jesus, after His resurrection, came to His disciples and blessed them with His peace. However, 'they were startled and frightened, thinking they saw a ghost. He said to them, "Why are you troubled, and why do doubts arise in your minds? Look at my hands and my feet. It is I myself! Touch me and see; a ghost does not have flesh and bones as you see I have."

When He had said this, He showed them His hands and feet. And while they still did not believe it because they were so overwhelmed with joy and amazement, He asked

63

them, "Do you have anything here to eat?" They gave Him a piece of broiled fish, and He took it and ate it in their presence.'

It is because of this that we dare to believe in the resurrection of the body. Jesus died; He was buried; His spirit and body were separated for three days and three nights. What happened on that first Easter morning was that what death had separated God brought together again in resurrection.

'Because I live, you shall live also', He cries – and this is the heart of the Christian Faith. If Jesus lived and died like any other great man, we do not have a Gospel to preach! But there is another event authenticated in history – His Resurrection!

The purpose of resurrection is judgment in the first instance. This is God's timetable – no doubt faithfully kept and faultlessly carried out. For this reason not only the good, but also the bad will be resurrected. Paul affirms this as he stands defending himself against the charge of sectarianism before the Governor Felix. Tertullus, that gifted and persuasive lawyer, had accused him of initiating an unregistered religion, a 'religio illicita' forbidden by the Roman authorities. 'I have the same hope in God as these men', declares Paul 'that there will be a resurrection of both the righteous and the wicked'. Whatever the Bible teaches about life after death it always divides it into two. Wherever you look in Scripture there is a constant distinction leading to the greatest divide of all – the gulf fixed between heaven and hell! There are two groups – and only two groups – so far as the Bible is concerned, the just and the unjust. The *just* are in the category of those who are worthy to live with God, His Son and His angels forever. To be included requires one of two things – perfection or pardon. To be perfect in the eyes of God is to have lived a life doing everything you should have done and doing nothing you should not have done. If that were the only way to heaven, then there would be only one person there – Jesus!

However, there is another way in the mercy of God – to be pardoned! The Bible puts millions of people in this category. The *unjust* are neither perfect nor pardoned, but they too will be resurrected. I sense that Jesus was aware of how strange this is to the human mind and heart – 'Do not be amazed at this,' He says, 'for a time is coming when all who are in their graves will hear his voice and come out – those who have done good will rise to live, and those who have done evil will rise to be condemned.' Solemn and alarming, but the words of the Son of God. God's timetable indicates that for the *just* resurrection will occur when Jesus Christ comes again in power and glory. '. . . our citizenship is in heaven. And we eagerly await a Saviour from there, the Lord Jesus Christ, who, by the power that enables him to bring everything under his control, will transform our lowly bodies so that they will be like his glorious body.' Writing to the Christians at Thessalonica, who were facing persecution from outside and confusion and uncertainty from within, Paul encourages and assures them in this way: 'For the Lord himself will come down from heaven, with a loud command, with the voice of the archangel and with the trumpet call of God, and the dead in Christ will rise first. After that we who are still alive and are left will be caught up with them in the clouds to meet the Lord in the air. And so we will be with the Lord forever.'

The return of Christ is the next great event in history. For every occasion the first coming of Christ (Christmas) is spoken of in the Bible there are eight occasions when His second coming is spoken of. There are over three hundred references to it in the New Testament, and twelve hundred in the Old Testament. It is to this, and for this, that every Christian looks. The Bible seems to indicate that the *unjust* will not be resurrected at the same time. There is clear evidence that resurrection is for everyone, but the *unjust* will be behind the *just*.

How will this happen? The answer to that question is difficult to verbalise. With the return of Christ you have to use the phrase: 'the same yet different'. His return will be the same as His first coming and yet so different. Jesus came to Bethlehem, so small, so weak, so humble. Hardly anyone knew that He was the King of Kings. His coming again will be like lightning blazing from east to west. When we ask the question: 'How will we rise from the dead?' the answer is the same as that i.e. 'the same yet different'. Our new bodies will be related unmistakably to our present bodies and yet they will be so vastly different. Only yesterday I stood before a crowded congregation in our local Crematorium Chapel. For the most part, not only was the funeral service strange to them, but the experience of being in church was unusual. The Christian Faith at the best of times was difficult for them to grasp and was certainly not part of their lives, but the categorical affirmation that the body of the deceased, about to be disintegrated by fire, would be resurrected at the coming of Christ was so far-fetched as to be laughable. I read a large section of Paul's First Letter to the Corinthians Chapter 15 from Kenneth Taylor's paraphrase in the Living Bible, where there is so much to help our understanding. The Bible counsels: 'Look in your garden to help you understand'. A seed potato planted will produce other potatoes very like the original, but quite different. However, a Kerr's Pink will remain a Kerr's Pink! We already have experience of how one body can change to another. It is always interesting to look at the photograph of the baby when you know the adult – and sometimes embarrassing too! I understand that my body anyway changes its cells every seven years. So apparently every seven years I get a refit. Perhaps the most powerful visual aid is the change from the caterpillar to the butterfly – one leads to a totally different dimension and environment of life. So with our bodies in resurrection. In that most remarkable chapter in the Bible on the nature of our resurrection body (1 Corinthians 15) Kenneth Taylor in his paraphrase of the Bible puts it this way:

First, then, we have these human bodies and later on God gives us spiritual, heavenly bodies. Adam was made from the dust of the earth, but Christ came from heaven above. Every human being has a body just like Adam's, made of dust, but all who become Christ's will have the same kind of body as His – a body from heaven. Just as each of us now has a body like Adam's, so we shall someday have a body like Christ's.

I can only assume that since the *just* will have a body which reflects the full glory of their real life in Christ, the *unjust* will have a body which reflects their real life without Christ. It is an awesome thought that in the pardoned sinner the real beauty of our Saviour will be shown, whilst in the unrepentant sinner the real horror of Satan will be seen. It is certainly logical that if resurrection brings the beauty of salvation to perfection, then it will also bring the ugliness of sin to perfection.

I have often stood in cemeteries – especially very old ones – and tried to imagine the scenes around some of these graves in years gone by. Now they are overgrown, sunken and neglected; the gravestone is all but wiped clean by generations of rain, sleet, snow and wind; the occupants long since forgotten, apart from an entry perhaps on the yellowed mildewed pages of a parish register. Perhaps even some of those who stood at that open grave one day broken-hearted, tearful, and bereft, hardly knowing how to face the future that lay bleakly ahead are themselves now its occupants. But their loved ones are long-since gone. Their descendants have moved to other parts – perhaps even to the other side of the world, and there lived out their span of years and been buried too. Grass, and weeds, and brambles, and time have completed their anonymity – but not to God! Death is not the end! However final, complete and absolute it may appear – death is not the end!

Years ago there was a great deal of speculation about a sea route to India in the political and economic circles in

European capitals. The question that was being asked was: 'Is there a way to the rich land of spices round the southern tip of Africa?' Those who had examined the situation suspected that there was. However, all brave attempts to round the southern tip of Africa – a treacherous headland where the Pacific and Atlantic Oceans meet – had failed so that it became known as the Cape of Storms. One intrepid sailor determined to try again. He succeeded and navigated that treacherous headland and reached the East. There is still a monument to this famous sailor, Vasco da Gama, in China today. Ever since he returned in triumph to Lisbon it has become quite impossible to doubt that a way to the East does exist round the southern part of Africa. Even the name of that terrible Cape was changed to its present title, the Cape of Good Hope.

The enigma of life after death is just like that. Until the time Jesus died and rose again, death was like that Cape of Storms, the place where hopes were wrecked, hearts were broken, and faith foundered. Until His successful rounding of that Cape and return, men had nothing to go on, but speculation about the after life. But the Easter joy of His resurrection has turned it into the Cape of Good Hope. He has opened up for His people the way to a new and rich land which He has shown exists. Because He has satisfactorily rounded that perilous Cape, He is well equipped to act as pilot to others. Christian certainty and optimism about the reality that death is not the end is not, as Bertrand Russell has said: 'Built on the ground that fairy-tales are pleasant', but is founded on the solid basis of the resurrection of Jesus Christ from the grave. C. S. Lewis in his book *Miracles* writes, 'He has forced open a door that has been locked since the death of the first man. He has met, fought, and beaten the King of Death. Everything is different because He has done so. This is the beginning of the new Creation: a new chapter in cosmic history has opened.'

Death is not the end! Beyond death there is not one destiny, but two.

5: Judgment – The bills have to be paid sometime

There is something beguiling in modern commerce which attempts to take the pain out of paying for goods or services already received and enjoyed. It may be by an instalment system or by a delayed payment – what you need or want you can have without the responsibility of paying for it now. It can be yours – you can possess it; enjoy it; let others admire it – without paying for it now! The vendor, however, is never the loser no matter how attractive and expansive his advertising – the goods have to be paid for by you sometime and the penalty for non-payment in full is written into the contract. In a sense judgment is a bit like that! The bills may not have to be paid every Friday, but they have to be paid. In human nature there is a mechanism which almost convinces us that if we can get away with it in this life we will never have to face it in the next. However, written clearly for us to read is the unassailable reality that the bills have to be paid sometime.

Although we may want to resist this reality – and even resent it – it is hard to see why this should be so. The necessity of judgment or accountability is built into the whole framework of our life. Each one of us is aware that we have to give an account of our time, work, money, or abilities to someone sometime. Is it then too radical a concept that a created being should give an account of his life to the one who created him – having given him resources and opportunities to live his life. Whatever the twentieth century will be remembered for, it must surely reflect a deep sense of justice. Few days pass without management and labour being in confrontation over wage claims. The media explores claim and counter-claim to the point of weariness. The conciliation service, ACAS, must surely be the best known institution in modern Britain, and its rather unimpressive front door just off the Thames embankment in West London the most frequented location by TV camera crews. All this is the modern paraphernalia to achieve justice. Everywhere today there is a clamour for justice – if it is not a wage claim, then it is an offended protest over racial discrimination or an indignant outcry over the West's insensitivity and selfishness towards the Third World. It is right that we should be concerned about these things – but God also demands justice. If we are concerned about justice, how much more so is God! There could be no goodness nor love of God without justice and judgment. If there were no justice, life would be a meaningless thing which leaves us confused and afraid in our most honest moments.

So the Bible affirms judgment from its beginning to its end. '. . . man is destined to die once, and after that to face judgment . . .'. Judgment is as sure as death.

I did a small part of my theological training in a denominational college in the centre of Glasgow. The building which housed the college in those days was dismal, decrepit and Victorian. It was approached by a winding stone staircase. There I made friendships which have lasted through the years and was constantly challenged by my own spiritual poverty in the face of the godliness of many of my peer group. The Principal of the college was a warm man, generous in hospitality, with an eccentric sense of humour. I can remember how his lectures were spiced with reminiscences and highland charm. One morning, before he got underway, with a fair flourish of authority he said: 'Gentlemen, if life is going to bring you peace of mind, you must learn to keep a diary. There are two things you must remember: always make sure that you put all your appointments in your diary and then always remember to read it.'

However, there are two appointments which none of us

can ever put in our diaries – one is the day we are going to die, and the other is the day we are going to be judged. Yet each one of us must keep both these appointments whether we possess a diary or not. There is a tendency to romanticise about life after death rather than face its realities and to sentimentalise about it rather than face up to what God has to say.

Judgment is necessary for two main reasons. *First* of all because of the injustice of this present life. Psalm 73 is the expression of the inner conflicts of a man's heart over a fundamental problem which has troubled many in every generation – why do the righteous suffer and the wicked prosper? There is clear evidence in many circumstances that the 'goodie' does not always win in the end, and the 'baddie' does not always get what he deserves. The Psalmist really struggles with this until he sees the present 'unfairness' of God in the light of eternity. It goes a long way to solving the mystery of suffering for him when the concept of judgment is included and he sees that right will be vindicated over wrong at last. Then the problem of injustice becomes less perplexing. This life is lived in a world full of suffering and sin and evil and violence and lust and greed, and taken by itself leaves injustice, unfairness and unbalance. Because life is as it is God demands the necessity of justice. There is something instinctive within all of us which feels that somewhere beyond death all will be put right. There is something rational within all of us which cannot accept that a Nero and a St Paul, an Adolf Eichman and an Albert Schweizer, an Adolf Hitler and a Martin Niemöller, an agnostic and a St Augustine, an atheist and an Athanasius, a Judas and a James can all equally be committed to the elements 'in the sure and certain hope of the resurrection to eternal life through Jesus Christ our Lord'.

Secondly judgment is necessary because of the justice of God. If God is good then He must put things right. If we say that life can be grossly unfair and unjust, and that God is good and just, then there must be an expression of God's justice beyond death if He is to be a good God. If there were no justice established in the future then it would raise insuperable problems in having convictions about a good God. In a variety of ways, however, the Bible repeatedly says and demonstrates that 'whatever a man sows in this life that he will also reap, because God is not mocked'.

With equal clarity God also indicates that there is nothing vague or tenuous about the occasion. Not only is judgment certain, but there will also be a day of judgment. 'For He has set a day when He will judge the world with justice by the man He has appointed. He has given proof of this to all men by raising Him from the dead.' Why should this be so? Why could we not be judged the day we died? Why wait for a final examination? Why wait till the resurrection of the dead? Simply because true justice will always be *public*. Justice must never be done in secret. Justice has to be seen to be right. So in this life the public gallery of the Law Courts is an important part of the whole proceedings. However painful and embarrassing the facts of the matter, they have to be disclosed for all to hear and consider. It would only be in the most exceptional cases that the media is barred. Sometimes public decency is offended by what comes to light and the worst aspects of human nature are fed, yet secret trials strike fear into fair-minded people. Countries where these take place are under the heel of a totalitarian regime. Secret trials take place because those in authority are afraid to allow people to see what is happening because they would see that it is not just. Justice must be *public* – and the Bible makes it clear that God's justice will always be just that! Why should this be so strongly stated? There are really three reasons for this.

First of all *God* must be vindicated. God must be seen to be just and fair. In this world many have taken umbrage at what God has allowed and done, and have been quick to declare that God is unfair and unjust. Often with regard to God the question 'why?' has been asked. There must be a day when God is unmistakably seen to be what He is – just and fair.

Secondly *Christ* must be vindicated. So far as the world is concerned, the last they saw of Him was when He hung upon a Roman gibbet exposed and naked. He had been condemned as an imposter, a lawbreaker, a criminal, an insurrectionist, guilty of blasphemy. However clearly Christian testimony has given the lie to these charges, the world at large is prone to believe that there is no smoke without fire.

And then thirdly *Christians* must be vindicated. Through the centuries they have appeared in a bad light – sometimes deserved, but not always! There has not been a period of ten years in the last two thousand years when Christians have not been martyred because they belong to Jesus. Their martyrdom has often been accompanied by spurious and trumped-up charges. There must be a day when they are clearly seen to be what they are – the people of God.

So a day of judgment – public for all to see – is written into the Bible. You cannot read the Bible without being aware of it – in the Old Testament prophets and the New Testament letters as well as the teaching of Jesus Christ. Jesus speaks clearly of a day when what has formerly been together will be separated so as to be clearly seen – the wheat will be separated from the tares; the sheep will be separated from the goats; the wise bridesmaids will be separated from the foolish ones.

On a number of occasions I have been present at a court hearing. There is a unique atmosphere prior to the proceedings beginning. Some appear to be relaxed and unconcerned, whilst others quite clearly are not so. It is rather like sitting in a doctor's waiting room and wondering what the others are there for. Some lounge, some smoke a cigarette casually, some read the newspaper, some sit and stare, some talk animatedly, some look uncomfortable and somewhat agitated, and some appear as if they have seen it all and done it all before. The air is pervaded by a sense of unreality. Then electricity sweeps through all who have gathered. The first case is about to be taken. Tension mounts, and there are some last minute, hurried conversations between lawyers and clients. The police on duty remain aloof and dispassionate. Whatever has been the matter under discussion – there is only one penetrating question now: 'Who is on the bench today?' 'Who is going to try me?' 'Who is going to take my case?' 'Who?'.

So with the day of judgment – who will judge me? The most obvious answer might well be that God will judge us. But, in fact, on that day God has delegated that responsibility to someone else – another human being. A man is going to judge mankind – someone who has known all the problems, the pressures, the troubles, the tensions and temptations which have confronted us. His name is Jesus. Jesus did not become a man just for thirty-three years only – but for all eternity. He will be on the bench. He will be our judge.

G. A. Studdert Kennedy, who was 'Woodbine Willie' the padre during World War One, in his *Rough Rhymes of a Padre*, puts these words into the mouth of a cockney soldier:

There ain't no throne, and there ain't no books,
    It's 'im you've got to see.
It's 'im, just 'im, that is the Judge
    Of blokes like you and me.
And boys I'd rather be frizzled up
    In the flames of a burning 'ell
Than stand and look into 'is face,
    And 'ear 'is voice say, 'Well!'

It is awe-inspiring that a day will come when not only I will stand before Jesus, but Jesus will confront Pontius Pilate in the dock. Those who have judged Jesus through the ages will stand and hear what He thinks and says to them. There is a verse of an old hymn which says with poor poetry, but with spiritual truthfulness:

Jesus is standing in Pilate's hall
    Friendless, forsaken, despised by all.
Hearken, what meaneth this sudden call:
    What will you do with Jesus?
What will you do with Jesus?
    Neutral you cannot be!
Someday your heart will be asking:
    What will He do with me?

It is easy to be interested in these things and to cast your eye over the details referring to judgment like a spectator in the public gallery of the Law Court. It is quite another thing to come to terms with the reality that one day you will be in the dock – for none is exempt. All human beings who have ever lived will be judged in one way or another. As you read these pages, you are reading of something in which one day you will be involved.

Back in 1917 the Annual Exhibition of the Royal Academy was held in London. Charles E. Butler exhibited a picture which has since become famous. He called it 'King of Kings'. He depicts Jesus standing at the foot of the Cross on Calvary receiving homage from the crowned heads of the world. It took Butler three years to complete his picture. His dying wish was that the painting should be taken from town to town and exhibited without charge to all who cared to come and see it. The Prince of Darkness cowers behind Christ while the monarchs of the world press in to do Him honour. Edward the Confessor kisses His pierced hand. Louis IX of France proffers his crown. Constantine, the first Christian Roman Emperor, kneels beside King Athelstan and King Cetewayo of Zululand finds his place beside Queen Victoria. Julius Caesar, the Emperor Barbarossa, Richard Cœur-de-Lion, and Napoleon are all prominent in the adoring multitude. In all there are 158 portraits of people and only two are not royal personages – George Washington and Oliver Cromwell.

As there is an acknowledgment of who is King so there

will be an acknowledgment of who is Judge – by commoners as well as kings; by the small as well as by the great; by the dead as well as by the living. Each person will be dealt with personally. It is difficult in our human way of thinking to know how this can possibly happen, although we do know that a thousand years in God's sight are as one day. However difficult to envisage – your turn will come. Anything less than that would be unjust. There will be mass judgment and punishment. When I was at school there was a form of discipline which I could never fully understand – that because of the misbehaviour of one member of the class, the whole class was punished. During wartime the same unjust principle has been practised – because of the treachery of a few within a community the whole community has been put to the sword or the fire or the bullet. It will not be like that at the last. It will be your life which will be under scrutiny. This should make us much more concerned about our own standards in attitude, motive and behaviour than anyone else's.

We will not be judged on that day on the basis of *appearance*. We are very prone to pass judgment on how things appear to be. But God will not be concerned with what seems to be from the outside, but rather with what really is on the inside – in my heart. Nor will I now be judged on what I *say*. Jesus made it clear that He will cut through the hymns we sing; the prayers we offer; the preaching we claim to love and identify as truth; the testimony we give when asked to give it. In an almost frightening passage Jesus says: 'Not everyone who says to me, "Lord, Lord", will enter the Kingdom of heaven, but only he who does the will of my father who is in heaven. Many will say to me on that day, "Lord, Lord, did we not prophesy in your name, and in your name drive out demons and perform many miracles?" Then I will tell them plainly, "I never knew you, away from me, you evildoers!" ' We have laid a great emphasis upon a profession of faith – but that is not where the Bible lays its emphasis. In what is perhaps the most ethically demanding book of the New Testament – the First Letter of John – the writer is anxious that we should not be beguiled by what we or anyone else says. Notice his early emphasis on the danger of the claims we make and the words we speak for profession without practice is spurious and faith without works is dead. There has to be visible, tangible evidence of the invisible reality which we claim. So how we seem to others and what we say of ourselves will not be the basis of judgment. Nor will the *testimony* of others on our behalf be valid. There may well be witnesses for the prosecution, but there will be no witnesses for the defence. God already knows all about us, and requires nothing from the lips of others.

Today a case can be dismissed in Court on the basis of a technicality of the law. But the law of God is perfect and will afford no loophole to ease the case.

Where will the evidence come from? What will be the basis of my case? John, in his vision in Revelation, says that he saw: '. . . the dead, great and small, standing before the throne, and books were opened. Another book was opened, which is the book of life. The dead were judged according to what they had done as recorded in the books.' So there are already completed biographies on the shelves of God's library awaiting the opening day. There you will find the life of Samuel Johnson, but so different from the one that James Boswell wrote; and there the life of Thomas Arnold, but not a bit like the one that came from Arthur Penryn Stanley; and there the life of Horatio Nelson, but such a contrast to the one which Robert Southey gave us. These famous biographers recorded all they could find of the good, and all too often they by-passed the bad; they had space only to speak of the more or less important things; they had because of circumstances to omit the insignificant; they did not, could not, pen the complete story. There, one day, our record will rest – containing the bad as well as the good; the insignificant as well as the important; the private as well as the public. Everything we have said and done;

every thought which has possessed our mind and every attitude which has motivated our actions. One day the books will be opened and the evidence in its entirety and accuracy produced.

We shall be judged by the standard of God. There are some laws which apply only to the people who accept them – these are laws of voluntary associations. These laws are made by people who associate themselves together in order to pursue some particular aim within a community. These may be the laws of a golf club or a dramatic society or a gardeners' association. No one is compelled to join – but if you do there are certain rules and regulations which must be observed. If you do not like them you can leave. If you do not observe them you are unacceptable within that group. However, within voluntary associations, the law only applies to those who want it to apply to them.

There are other laws which vary with different localities. It is a crime, for example, in some parts of Switzerland to cut down your own tree without planting two others; it is not a crime in England. Another example of this is that when America was 'dry', many Americans living near the Canadian border made a practice of going across the border to get a drink. Prohibition did not apply in Canada, but it did in America. You could drink there with impunity.

Yet again, there are laws which alter with the passing of time – what is law in one generation is not necessarily in another. For example, in England at the time of John Wesley there were 160 different crimes for which men, women, and children could be hanged. There are none today. In those days you could be hanged if you picked a pocket of more than five pence; if you grabbed goods from someone's hands and ran away with them; if you took from a store goods valued at more than twenty-five pence; if you stole a horse, or a sheep, or even ensnared a rabbit on a gentleman's estate. Charles Wesley records in one place in his Journal that he was preaching in a prison to fifty-two prisoners who were waiting to be hanged – and one of them was a little boy of ten. There is an almost unbelievable story from the early history of the white settlements of South Africa. There were some strange and eccentric characters there. One of these was a man called Ikey Sonnenberg. Ikey ran a store which catered for the needs of the Boers. Many of these were simple and pious men whom Ikey did not find it difficult to deceive. On one occasion one of these Boers was selling his wool to Ikey. The wool bales were weighed and the price fixed at three pence per pound. Ikey made a quick calculation and announced that the total came to £153. The Boer farmer consulted his Ready Reckoner and said: 'No; according to my Ready Reckoner the total is £173 4s 3d.' Ikey seized the Ready Reckoner and examined it quickly, and then exclaimed: 'Good heavens, you're using last year's Ready Reckoner. It is worthless this year!' The old Boer accepted the explanation and received the lesser amount Ikey was prepared to pay. In our much more sophisticated society we would not be so gullible, because what was true yesterday in arithmetic is true also today.

So there are human laws of voluntary associations which apply only to those who freely accept them. There are human laws which apply in one location, but not in another. And there are human laws which are relevant at one time in history, but not in another. But the laws of God are not like these human laws. The human race is not a voluntary association. We are born, without our choice, in a way the Creator devised, into a family life which He planned, and under conditions which He laid down. It is not possible to withdraw from human association – though many have tried. Nor does God have one law for those living in America and a quite different law for those living in Russia. Whatever may be true of the laws and customs of nations, the law of the Lord does not vary with locality. His law applies whether we like it or not, and His law applies everywhere; among the Pygmies and the Eskimos; at the Equator and in Antarctica; in the palace and in the slum.

And, of course, the laws of God never change. They have been the same in every age. The Factory Acts may need to be revised and Capital Punishment may be debated as a matter of conscience in the House of Commons, but the Ten Commandments and the other six hundred and thirteen laws of God which go along with them never change. They are eternal, written in the Heavens, and binding on all generations. Every age makes its effort to subvert them, but these efforts have no effect upon their sublime truth. Still the law of God stands and ultimately vindicates itself. Men seem to break it, but, in the end, it breaks them.

We shall each, then, be judged according to how much of the revealed will of God we know. It would be unjust for God to judge someone on the basis of something they never knew. We have, however, an absolute assurance in the Bible that such a thing will never happen (cf. Romans 2). Everyone will be judged according to the light they have received – but God's standard does not alter.

On this basis there are three significant groups in the human race.

The *first group* comprises those who have heard about Jesus Christ, the Son of God, and Christian standards of truth. This group will be judged according to Jesus Christ and His Gospel and the standards which He set before us. There are many who consider themselves to be Christians, but ministers, pastors, priests and vicars will be judged for withholding the truth from them. The Gospel which has been committed to the Church has so often been emaciated through the rationalism and humanism and self-interest of those who have shared it. This first group often appears to get concerned about those who have never heard. It may well be our responsibility to ensure that others do hear the liberating good news of the love and sheer undeserved generosity of God – but what happens to those who do not can be safely left in the strong and just hands of God.

The *second group* comprises the Jewish nation. They have

been very specially favoured by God and have been given the Ten Commandments. According to these they will be judged, since every Jew has had the Ten Commandments.

The *third group* comprises those who remain outside the first two groups. They have never heard the gospel of our Lord Jesus Christ nor have they been given the Ten Commandments. However, they have had two things from God which have clearly revealed His will to them. They themselves are part of God's creation and live in a world which God has created. Inevitably by looking around them at the created world at the things God has made they should be aware that there is a power greater than themselves which should tell them that there is one to whom they should bow. So they have the created world around them. The other thing which God has given them is a conscience — God's revelation within them. This is the God-given ability to distinguish between right and wrong. Conscience cannot be explained away on the basis of social convention or tribal custom, since often those in whom conscience has operated most powerfully have run counter to social convention and broken out of tribal custom.

This third group then will be judged according to the light they have received by means of creation around them and conscience within them. The philosopher, Immanuel Kant, declared 'two things fill me with increasing wonder and awe: the starry heavens above me, and the moral law within me.'

God's standard then will ask how we have been relating to *Him* and to *one another* on the basis of the light and understanding we have had. The real problem which confronts the human race is that no one — in whatever group he is to be found — can say with honesty: 'I have always lived up to the light I have had.' The Christian is unable to declare that he has always pursued the truth as Jesus has shared it; the Jew, however devout, can never claim to have kept all the Commandments; and the remainder cannot affirm that they have always responded to the promptings of conscience. The real fact of the matter is that while the Bible affirms that we will be judged according to the light we have – our hearts affirm that by that light we all stand guilty before God. If each of us had lived up to the light we have then, of course, there is nothing to fear in God's judgment. However, none has done that. It is for this reason that the Church in every generation has been concerned to send the Gospel of Jesus Christ throughout its neighbourhood and to the furthest places of the earth. If people were in a state of innocence before God then to take the Gospel to them would damn them. But wherever men are found, and to whatever group they belong, they already have the light and have not lived up to it and so desperately need forgiveness.

Yet the Bible clearly declares that a great number of people will be acquitted – in fact they will never reach the dock. These are people who are not to be condemned! Why should this be?

There is another Book that has already been spoken of – the Lamb's Book of Life. It belongs to Jesus, and only He can write in it. It contains the names of those who have asked their case to be taken earlier. They have asked God deliberately not to wait until the Day of Judgment to deal with their sin. It is not that they are confident about their innocence, but rather they are convicted by their sin. However, they recognise that this is what Good Friday, and the Cross of Christ is all about – that because Jesus, the Son of God, died in their place they might be justified, freely forgiven and so acquitted. God has found a way whereby His *justice* and His *mercy* can be satisfied together.

There is a church in York which has a tablet inside which commemorates a certain Canon Faussett, who, like a number of clergy in his day, owned land in Ireland. During the potato famine in Ireland some families in his estates were unable to pay their rents to him. They wrote to the worthy Canon, begging to be let off from meeting their debt. He replied that he could not possibly do this since it would be wrong and set up a bad precedent, and so there could be no exceptions. He insisted that everyone must pay their bills to the last penny. In each letter of reply from him, however, he enclosed a slip of paper. It was a cheque which was more than sufficient to pay all that they owed him.

This is a tiny and inadequate picture of what God has accomplished in Christ on the Cross for us, in order that we might be forgiven and His justice might be satisfied. This is why Paul writes in ecstacy to the Christians in Colossae; 'You were dead in sins, and your sinful desires were not yet cut away. Then He gave you a share in the very life of Christ, for He forgave all your sins, and blotted out the charges proved against you, the list of His commandments which you had not obeyed. He took this list of sins and destroyed it by nailing it to Christ's Cross.' God does not minimise sin or overlook it, but He does deal with it.

I do not stand a chance on the Day of Judgment on the basis of all that is in my life. But as I acknowledge what God has done for me in Christ and ask that God will take my case now on that basis – then He will, and my name will then be written in the Lamb's Book of Life.

This raises one final question – does this mean, then, that Christians will not be judged later since their judgment has been taken at the Cross? The answer is 'No' and 'Yes'. 'No' insofar as they will not face punishment for their sin, since that has already been dealt with. But 'Yes' insofar that Jesus will test their service for Him on the basis of how we have used the resources and the opportunities He has made available. This judgment will not prevent us going to heaven, but will be for the purpose of reward and position when we get there! Our position and responsibilities in heaven will depend on our use of the opportunities we have taken on earth and the resources of God we have used to meet them. The principles which will operate for the Christian will be the principles which operate at the Chelsea Flower Show rather than the principles which operate at the Old Bailey.

6: Hell – The real terror

The first time I ever consciously visited Dundee in the mid-east of Scotland there were only two things which interested me about that fine city. One was the railway bridge which spanned the River Tay leading to the southern approach to the city, and the other was the Church of St Peter. My interest in the bridge stemmed from accounts I had heard from my parents as a little boy of the train disaster which occurred one night in a fearful storm – an incident which obviously had stunned the whole of Scotland. My interest in the church was born having read the Memoirs and Remains of Robert Murray McCheyne which had been gathered by Andrew Bonar. This book has remained a constant companion to me through the years and from it I have drawn a great deal of inspiration. Murray McCheyne became the minister of St Peter's, and there God used him in a remarkable way. It is said that this young man once asked God for a vision of hell and God in His wisdom gave him what he asked for. Whenever Robert Murray McCheyne preached on this theme after this experience, he always wept and tears stained the carved pulpit. The impact of the awfulness and reality of hell so stirred him that he was unable to hide his reaction to it. Perhaps my interest in Dundee was somewhat macabre, but I have reflected in subsequent years that the first interest represents potential human disaster whilst the other represents potential human destiny.

General Booth, the founder of the Salvation Army, without McCheyne's vision, was nevertheless impressed by the awfulness of hell as he read of it in the Bible. Addressing cadets of the Salvation Army in the training college with typical practicality, he said: 'I would rather take you for two days into hell than have you spend two years in a Bible College.' He judged that the impact would be so profoundly stirring that it would provide a stimulus to do the primary job of the Salvation Army—preach the reality of God's salvation in Jesus Christ. Since it was not possible to do the former he obviously settled for the latter. Again, however, there was the practical impressiveness of the reality of hell, which stirred this man to confront a whole range of social abuses which soiled the society of his day. No one would argue that there was very little obscurantism about William Booth. He once said you can never warm a man's heart when his feet are cold.

Twentieth century man particularly has recoiled from the whole concept of hell as being too bizarre and contradictory to the reality that God is a God of love. To man's struggles with the idea of hell C. S. Lewis responds: 'In the long run the answer to all those who object to the doctrine of hell is itself a question: "What are you asking God to do?" To wipe out their past sins and, at all costs, to give them a fresh start, smoothing every difficulty and offering every miraculous help? But He has done so on Calvary.'

Hell is an Anglo-Saxon word which really means a hidden or a dark place. It was used to describe the space under a tailor's bench where he threw his rubbish and scraps of material for which he never would have any further use. In a rather more tender way it was used for a secret place which two lovers had found and which they used for meeting together so as not to be seen. According to the general teaching, however, of the New Testament the only definition which will fit the facts related to it there is that it is a place of conscious torment where the wicked will be punished forever. The awesomeness of such a definition has inevitably caused strong and persistent reaction. Unable to cope with its implication man, particularly in the nineteenth and twentieth centuries, has rejected the whole idea of hell with little attempt to explore its challenge rationally. McNeill Dixon makes a very significant

85

observation on this. He says: 'The kind-hearted humanitarians of the nineteenth century decided to improve on Christianity. The thought of hell offended their susceptibilities. They closed it, and to their surprise the gates of heaven closed also with a melancholy bang. The malignant countenance of Satan disturbed them. They dispensed with him and at the same time God took His departure.'

It would be important to look candidly at some of the reasons why there has been such a strong reaction to hell in view of the fact that 'the reality and eternity of suffering in Gehenna is an element of Biblical truth that an honest exegesis cannot evade'. The fact is that, on the one hand, God is omnipotent and God is love, and, on the other, eternal retribution is plainly taught in Scripture.

Sentiment forms a significant factor in rejecting the concept of hell. There are many facts and features of life which I do not like – and so I close my mind to them. They are too painful and far-reaching in their demands – and so I refuse to think them through clearly so that I need not take any action or make any response. On this shaky foundation I can convince myself, and sometimes others too, that I do not believe this. In reality what I am saying is: 'I do not like this!' Sentiment and feelings, however, play havoc with the facts of the matter.

Others reject hell on *psychological* grounds – it produces a strong reaction of fear, and fear is an unhealthy motive, and so fear ought not to be used. The conclusion is reached that the idea of hell which is bound to produce fear must be wrong. Fear, however, when based on reality, can be healthy. Indeed, historically, it has been a faithful servant of mankind in the development of the human race. It warns against danger and checks impetuosity. It begets a proper care, and compels caution and so can preserve life. Fear, indeed, is the most efficient policeman on our crowded roads and congested streets. No man is born without fear. Should such a person be born he would be a danger to the whole community and an object of dread. Fear, of course, can become a phobia, and in so doing it paralyses action and becomes unhealthy so that the person obsessed with this phobia cannot think of anything else. This psychological objection to hell has stopped preachers preaching about it more than any other for fear of manipulating the human personality and sending the hearers into a neurotic or psychotic state.

Social grounds have caused some to reject the idea of hell. Within society we no longer believe in the idea of retribution – punishment for its own sake. Where punishment is thought to be permissible it would normally be on the grounds that it acts as a deterrent or gives an incentive to reform. It is quite obvious that hell is so ultimate that it does neither. So if on sociological grounds we do not believe in punishment for its own sake – how could God be less humane than we are?

Still others have been disturbed by the *moral* implications of hell. It seems quite unjust that for a few sins of a comparatively short life a man is punished eternally – the punishment does not seem to fit the crime. It is extravagant and exorbitant in the light of the fault.

Perhaps a little more far-reaching is the *philosophical* objection to hell. If hell is necessary, then God has failed, and evil is eternal. Since God has failed to deal with and remove evil, it must be as everlasting as He is – and surely this cannot be?

The final objection to hell is the most frequently stated – it is the *theological* objection. If God is a God of love, how could He ever under any circumstances send anyone to hell? This surely would be a denial of His love! This often has been the ground on which the Church itself has shrouded and even denied the reality of hell. Significantly every one of the Cults has attacked the idea of hell and dismissed it. One of the characteristics of a Cult is its denial of basic Christian belief. It will challenge the heart of the Christian Faith – that Jesus is both God and man. It will teach that Jesus was a great medium, or a great leader, or a great prophet – but not both God and man. Or again, the Cults will challenge the Christian teaching on the Trinity; most Cults are unitarian and speak of God in terms of 'the life force', 'the eternal consciousness', and so on; usually with little reference to Jesus Christ. The whole concept of sin, and the atonement, and the need for repentance are almost always entirely missing. The emphasis is: 'Believe in yourself, you are wonderful if only you realised it. The concept of sin is an insult; it is simply psychological.' Now, if you really believe that, there is no need of Christ, there is no need for the Cross, there is no need for salvation, there is no need for New Birth, there is no need for repentance; judgment goes, hell goes and, of course, with it goes heaven too.

In the face of such strong opposition to the reality of hell what do you put in its place in the light of the references to it in the teaching of Jesus? It would be cavalier simply to ignore it. There are basically three alternatives to accepting its forthright implications in the New Testament.

First of all that hell is *self-imposed suffering in this life*. That would be the most popularly held view by Mr Everyman. You make your own hell here and it has nothing to do with life after death. After all, the circumstances of this life can often be painful enough and hard to endure. But God does not send a man to hell afterwards – you put yourself there now. Hell is something of your own making – and presumably of your own unmaking too! Unfortunately this view does not take into account the very pressing reality that there are people whose present circumstances are 'hellish', but they appear to be quite undeserved and beyond the persons ability or opportunity to do anything about them. Conversely there are those whose guile and wickedness and selfishness and arrogance would seem to warrant some kind of retribution, but they appear to live free from any significant adversity.

Secondly it is claimed that at some future date *God will save everybody*. This at least does acknowledge life after death in a way which the former view does not. This alternative is most commonly taught in churches where the biblical view has been rejected. It states that somehow, and at some time, God will find a way to achieve universal salvation – everyone will come to God some day, if not in this life, then in the next. This does, however, create a serious problem with regard to man's freedom. If one of the basic features of our humanity is our freedom to choose for ourselves, and God forces everyone at last to come to heaven, then He is no longer treating us like the beings He created us to be.

The *third* alternative to the Biblical teaching on hell is that *immortality is conditional* – only the righteous will live forever whilst the wicked will be extinguished and annihilated. Good will live on, but evil will cease to be. Some men are convinced they would prefer total extinction to the concept of heaven. The idea of an endless existence with God and His people is horrifying to them. Much better that the end of life on this earth is the end of life.

It is time to look more carefully at what the Bible actually has to say about hell, and its implications for us now. When honest investigation is carried out the first surprising thing is that there is hardly anything about hell in the Old Testament. In general terms the Old Testament is thought to be the severe part of the Bible – God is often portrayed as a God of war and punishment there. At the same time the New Testament is regarded as the pleasant and attractive part of the Bible – God is most clearly seen there as a God who loves and forgives. Whilst these generalisations are not strictly accurate, nevertheless this is the impression that is often held. In fact a doctrine of hell could not be built on the Old Testament. There is quite a lot about Sheol or Hades – the world of departed spirits – in the Old Testament, but little about hell itself.

The same would be true about another significant part of the Bible – the Letters of the New Testament. Again this is surprising since there is a general reaction that Paul, in particular, took the 'nice' religion of Jesus and added a lot of Jewish strictness to it.

Investigation, however, will reveal the true fact – most of what we know about hell comes from the lips of Jesus. For example the greatest love verse in the Bible clearly implies the possibility of appalling judgment – 'For God so loved the world that He gave His one and only Son, that whoever believes in Him shall not perish, but have eternal life.' If everything Jesus said about hell were to be removed there would be little left.

Why should this be so? Presumably because the whole concept of hell is so terrible and inconceivable to man that God wanted it to come from His Son direct. It is too deep a reality to be entrusted to anyone else. It is as if God were saying: 'I want you to hear this from someone who is more loving and more merciful and kind than anyone else since I doubt that you would believe it from anyone else.' Each of us has formed a general impression about the strictness of others like a Jeremiah or a Paul. We also have a general impression of Jesus.

Most of the teaching about hell comes in the first three Gospels – from the lips of Jesus there. It is dishonest and lacking in integrity to receive some of what Jesus said, and reject what does not suit us. Unless He is a downright liar or a disorientated lunatic I cannot pick and choose what I like and embrace that and decide what is distasteful and unacceptable to me and dismiss that. For example Jesus said: 'Do not be afraid of those who kill the body, but cannot kill the soul. Rather, be afraid of the one who can destroy both soul and body in hell.' Again, as recorded in Dr Luke, Jesus spoke clearly of hell: 'But I will show you whom you shall fear; fear him who, after killing the body, has power to throw you into hell. Yes, I tell you, fear him.'

From these two parallel passages there are five things about hell which are important to notice. First of all He uses the word Gehenna (Greek = GEENNA). This is the name given to the valley of Hinnom—a deep valley which runs round two sides of Jerusalem. It is deep and dark, and indeed there is a point where the sun never shines. Historically, this shady valley at one time was the place where the kings of Israel had their summer residences. It then became a place of culture where music was made. From that status it began to degenerate and became a place of pagan worship where shrines were erected and black magic and occult practices were carried out. It degenerated so far that it became defiled by human sacrifice to pagan gods as parents burned their own children. It was left to the young King Josiah to stop these practices and forbid that anyone should live there. Subsequently the valley of Hinnom became the rubbish dump of Jerusalem—everything that was useless was thrown over the wall of Jerusalem. Rapidly two things happened—worms and maggots ate what was edible and bonfires were kept going to destroy the rest.

In the time of Jesus the bodies of criminals were thrown into that valley—and the body of Jesus would have been thrown there had not Joseph of Arimathea intervened by providing a burial place in the garden which he owned. It was, however, in that valley that Judas hanged himself and went to his own place.

When Jesus, then, spoke of hell He always used this word—Gehenna. It is a very vivid picture—associated with darkness, perversion, rubbish, destruction, sin, rebellion and crime.

Secondly, Jesus speaks about the soul and the body separately in this context. He is referring to something which occurs *after* the body and the soul have been re-united in resurrection. He is urging that our fears are not to be misplaced. There are many who imagine that the death of the body is the worst possible thing which can happen to a man. Not so, says Jesus, there is something even worse which can happen to body and soul later.

Thirdly, Jesus uses the word 'destroy' for the event of hell. Our normal concept of that word is 'to obliterate'.

However, there is general agreement among scholars that what it really refers to is something which is ruined or wasted – something which has become useless. It is used in the Bible, for example, of the lost sheep in the famous story which Jesus told, and the ointment which the woman poured out on Jesus and which He appreciated so much, and which Judas condemned as wasteful. It is used of the withered wineskin which was unable to contain the new wine. Perhaps the best translation of the word is 'to perish'. We use that word of a bicycle or a car tyre or a hot-water bottle – it is perished! We do not mean that any of these things have ceased to be or have gone out of existence. We do mean that they have become useless for the purpose for which they were created. What do you do with a tyre or a hot-water bottle which has 'perished'? You put it in the dust-bin or the rubbish pile. Gehenna, then, was full of perished stuff – this is hell. But Jesus can mend broken lives. The thing which filled Him with horror was not that lives were broken and wasted, but that lives which could be mended and restored were perishing!

Fourthly, who is the *Him* whom we have to fear? Some have mistakenly concluded that Jesus is here referring to the devil. This, of course, is not so since the devil is himself to be destroyed. Jesus is referring here to God. Hell is not something which I make for myself – it is something which God is going to do. However unpleasant and difficult this may be for us to receive, the Bible is quite clear on this as it records the teaching of Jesus.

An Australian doctor, John Hercus, puts it very shrewdly:

The truth is that men never really have any problem, never any real problem, in understanding the strong, awesome judgment of God. They may complain about it, but they have no difficulty at all in understanding the ruthless judgment that declares that black is black because only the purest white is white. True, we hear from right, left and centre, from ignorant pagans, and even from highly trained theologians, the ignorant prattle about 'all this hellfire and brimstone talk isn't my idea of God. I think God is a God of love and I don't think He'd hurt a fly!' But it is easy to know why they talk like that; it's because they are terrified of the alternative.

Fifthly, there is clear and specific urging by Jesus that we are to be afraid of God who has the power to send man to hell forever. If it is psychologically bad for us to fear why did Jesus tell us to do so—after all He came to make us whole, not to cause our personality to disintegrate. There are realities where a good and healthy response is to fear—hell is one of these realities. This will not be to our detriment, but to our safety and our joy.

So far we have looked at only one part of the teaching of Christ on hell. Elsewhere He says: 'If your hand causes you to sin, cut it off. It is better for you to enter life maimed than with two hands to go into hell, where the fire never goes out. And if your foot causes you to sin, cut it off. It is better for you to enter life crippled than to have two feet and be thrown into hell. And if your eye causes you to sin, pluck it out. It is better for you to enter the Kingdom of God with one eye than to have two eyes and be thrown into hell, where

"their worms do not die, and the fire is not quenched".'

Jesus is saying that in this valley the worm does not die and the fires never go out. Although in the geographical valley of Hinnom this is not so today—in hell it is so. The worm never ceases in its perpetual scavenging and the fire never stops in its continual burning. This eliminates the conclusions of conditional immortality which we looked at earlier.

Again Jesus speaks of a dramatic separation at the last.

There is no question of all having the same final destiny. When this final separation occurs He says: 'Then He will say to those on his left, "Depart from Me, you who are cursed, into the eternal fire prepared for the devil and his angels . . . Then they will go away to eternal punishment, but the righteous to eternal life".' The staggering keynote in this part of His teaching is embodied in the word 'eternal'. The whole weight of Biblical evidence is that eternal means 'endless' – it never ceases! So the Bible speaks of God being eternal; and Christ being eternal; and salvation being eternal; and heaven being eternal. Frankly we cannot have it both ways – if eternal means temporary so far as hell is concerned so also it must mean temporary so far as heaven is concerned.

Those who react most strongly to this aspect of Jesus' teaching about hell have in their minds those horrific and grotesque medieval pictures of tortured bodies writhing in a furnace. In fact the artists' impressions only serve to obscure the real teaching of Christ, and, even more important, do not begin to convey the true severity of hell.

This is far greater and more solemn than that of a furnace or any such thing. Dr J. I. Packer has explained some of the terms which Jesus used when He taught, soberly and deliberately, about hell:

The 'worm' that 'dieth not' (Mark 9:48), an image, it seems, for the endless dissolution of the personality by a condemning conscience; 'fire' for the agonising awareness of God's displeasure; 'outer darkness' for knowledge of the loss, not merely of God, but of all good, and everything that made life seem worth living; 'gnashing of teeth' for self-condemnation and self-loathing. These things are, no doubt, unimaginably dreadful, though those who have been convicted of sin know a little of their nature. But they are not arbitrary afflictions; they represent rather a conscious growing into the state in which one has chosen to be. Nobody stands under the wrath of God save those who have chosen to do so. The essence of God's action in wrath is to give men what they choose in all its implications . . . God is hereby doing no more than to ratify and confirm judgments which those whom He 'visits' have already passed on themselves by the course they have chosen to follow.

There is at least one more significant thing that we need to grasp from Jesus' teaching on hell. He said: 'There will be weeping there, and gnashing of teeth when you see Abraham, Isaac and Jacob and all the prophets in the Kingdom of God, but you yourselves thrown out.' Quite obviously, the implication is that in hell you can see heaven, but not vice versa. That is certainly true of the valley of Gehenna. From the valley you can see the city of Jerusalem – in the ancient world a by-word for justice and fairness; the law court of the world – but you cannot see the valley properly from the city. Many who visit the Holy Land will stand and walk within half a mile of the valley of Hinnom and yet be unaware of its existence.

This is a quite terrifying concept – to begin to realise that forever you are excluded, left outside!

From this teaching certain things are absolutely clear. Hell is in the life after this life, not in this life here and now. It is not of our making, but of God's – no matter how responsible we are for the painful circumstances of this life. It is quite impossible to believe that all one day will experience heaven in the light of what we have looked at. Not only does Jesus deny this in His teaching on hell, but He also affirms this strongly in His teaching contained in the Sermon on the Mount and in a number of His parables. Hell is not just a possibility or a probability, but a certainty. Finally, some of the teaching on hell could be interpreted as total annihilation, but by no means all, for conscious continuation of life is clearly taught.

Most important in the light of this teaching is not just

95

that we have a clearer understanding (important as that undoubtedly is!), but that we make a realistic personal response to it. What we have been thinking of is not something to write about or read about or argue about – it is something which evokes a personal response now. If this is all true then it has the most profound practical implications which cannot be laid aside.

John Wesley and Charles Spurgeon and many, many others have pleaded with people to acknowledge their sin before God and respond to what He has done in Christ for them – in order that they would be saved from hell. Although this is not the primary motive for sharing the Gospel of Christ, yet it is an important one. It is not just the Neros or the Adolf Hitlers of this world who go to hell, but the man who has good intentions, but has never done anything to implement them. And so I join with many godly men and women down the centuries and urge you to receive what I am writing not simply in an academic way, but in an urgent personal way, and do something about it now. 'For God so loved the world that He gave His one and only Son, that whoever believes in Him shall not perish, but have eternal life. For God did not send His Son into the world to condemn the world, but to save the world through Him. Whoever believes in Him is not condemned, but whoever does not believe stands condemned already because he has not believed in the name of God's one and only Son.'

It is a great personal heartache that over the years since my ordination to the ministry there has been a continuing increase in interest in feeding minds and caring for bodies and a continuing decline in interest in saving lives for eternity. It is not that the former is unimportant, or unnecessary, but rather that the latter is of prime importance.

7: Heaven – Home at last!

Heaven is a word which evokes a sentimental response from the heart and often an unrealistic comment from the mind and yet there are three reasons why it will never pass from our vocabulary. First of all because there is something in man which earth can never satisfy – no matter how warm his relationships, distinguished his career or obvious his ability. Although we may feel that if only we had more of this and less of that we would be satisfied, in our heart of hearts we know that this is an illusion. William Watson, in his poem *World-Strangeness*, asked:

> In this house with starry dome,
>   Floored with gem-like plains and seas,
> Shall I never feel at home,
>   Never wholly be at ease?

Never! You were not meant to. Secondly, because there is in man instinctively a nostalgia for heaven – even where religious conviction has long since been overlaid or dismissed by a multitude of factors. 'Nostalgia' comes from two Greek words: 'nostos', which means 'return home'; and 'algos', which means 'pain'. Nostalgia originally meant that homesickness was an incurable malady; incurable that is by anything except home itself.

Dr W. E. Sangster tells how an alcoholic came into Westminster Central Hall one day while he was minister there, and as a result committed his life to Jesus Christ in a living relationship. Twenty years previously that man had been a church leader in the Midlands, but had come to London, took to drink, and deteriorated rapidly. His confrontation and commitment to Christ seemed to him to hold out an immediate cure for his problem. While that is the beginning of hope there are other ministries which God has given to His Body on earth to encourage, strengthen and stabilise those who are struggling. So there began that day, when he surrendered to Christ, a long guerilla warfare in his soul between the destructive craving and the reality of his new life in Christ. Dr Sangster, with typical compassion, encouraged him to drop in any day when he found the struggle especially hard. He came often – and on one occasion when they were praying together the contrast between his earlier life and the degradation and deception to which his alcoholism had brought him overwhelmed him and he sobbed like a child:

I know I'm in the gutter. I know it. But, Oh! . . .
I don't belong there, do I? Tell me, I don't belong
there . . .

William Sangster tells how, even in the embarrassment of this man's tears, he felt great elation. He was aware that although this man had lost his way . . . he had not lost his address. So he said to him quite positively:

You don't belong there . . . you belong to God. At the last, heaven is your home.

Thirdly, heaven is not a figment of man's imagination or a spurious flight into a world of fantasy, but is a reality promised by God and provided for in His eternal purposes. In 1543, Copernicus published his famous 'De Revolutionibus Orbium' in which he claimed that the earth, far from remaining motionless at the centre, actually travelled round the sun. The full implications of this theory were not grasped at once, but from the start it became crystal clear that this little planet on which we mortals live was robbed of its position of unique and unrivalled importance in the galaxy. As a result Copernicus was maligned and persecuted by his contemporaries, but truth has won the day and history has vindicated to the full the truth which he proclaimed. Any system of thought, political, scientific, economic or theological that opposes the truth is under sentence of death. The truth may be thwarted and perverted by evil men and even opposed by well-meaning men. For whole generations, even centuries, it may be driven underground, but in the end it is always irresistible. This is why Jesus is as much at home in the age of the atom and the micro-chip as He was in rural Palestine – He is the truth and the truth is indestructible.

This is why heaven will remain a reality – even though it is laughed at and dismissed by many – because it is a reality. This is why many in the darkness and bewilderment of bereavement have turned to the words of Jesus rather than the comfortless, though well-meaning, platitudes of men, for Jesus said clearly:

> Do not let your hearts be troubled. Trust in God; trust also in me. In my Father's house are many rooms; if it were not so, I would have told you. I am going there to prepare a place for you. And if I go and prepare a place for you, I will come back and take you to be with me that you also may be where I am.

There are two main opposing responses to the reality of heaven. There are those who are convinced that heaven is a *delusion*. In the days when Jesus Christ was on earth this response was expressed by a group of Jews called the Sadducees. They really struggled with the reality of life after death. No doubt there were others who could not verbalise their doubts so clearly. To the Sadducees Jesus said three things were responsible for their difficulties (Matthew 22:23–33). *Firstly*, He said, you have a problem because you try to imagine heaven in human and earthly terms. Now that is natural and in a sense inevitable, but it will always lead to a wrong conclusion. When heaven is spoken of we are immediately thrust into an area where we have no human terms of reference, so human concepts and vocabulary do not apply because Heaven is so completely different from earth that it is beyond not only our thought, but also our imagination. *Secondly*, you substitute childhood fantasy and adult fiction for Biblical teaching. There are literally hundreds of references to heaven in both the Old Testament and the New Testament. It is easy to settle for human sentiment and desire rather than the truth of God since the latter challenges us to faith as well as to reason. *Thirdly*, Jesus said, you do not really appreciate the reality of the power of God. If we could in some small measure realise the power of God at work making a world for this life, how much more will He provide a heaven for the next. Long before the world was created God had people in His heart. Before He formed the earth people were dear to Him and so He created a place suitable for these people to dwell. Because of His concern for those whom He wanted to love He made a world suited to their needs. How perfectly and abundantly He did this – with an attention to minute detail which is absolutely staggering. If we struggle over the reality of heaven it is because we struggle over the reality of the power of God.

Some years ago I went to West Africa for the first time. I travelled north from the Gulf of Guinea through Ghana and then west into Ivory Coast. I continued north there until we came to a community at the edge of very rough, uncultivated jungle terrain. While I was there I met a young African called Tilkaane. He was being cared for by two missionaries with whom I was staying. I got to know him. He was intrigued by the way I spoke and the way I dressed and by the few possessions I had with me – white men were a bit of a rarity in that part of the world. His French, although much better than mine, was somewhat stilted. He really spoke the Loron language, and it was difficult to communicate. However, with the help of one or both of the missionaries we managed reasonably well. In our times together Tilkaane would often dissolve into uncontrollable laughter as I tried to describe the London Underground system, or multi-storey flats, or television – some of the very familiar features of our western way of life which we take for granted. It was for him so unrelated to his experience that it was ridiculous and ludicrous. At that time he had travelled only a few miles from his own jungle community. He was a highly intelligent lad, but faced with realities totally unrelated to his experience he could only laugh at their apparent absurdity. I sense that for all of us we struggle in a similar way with what God says to us about heaven.

The other opposing response to heaven is that it is a *drug*. An Anglican clergyman, Charles Kingsley, was the first to use the phrase: 'religion is the opiate of the people'. Kingsley was deeply troubled by the social abuses of his day and was concerned about religious people who became so absorbed with heaven that they did little or nothing about the pressing needs and problems of earth. For example, he wrote the book 'The Water Babies' out of his indignation that little children were exploited by men without any regard to their health and safety. That particular book highlights the plight and pathos of chimney sweep children. Karl Marx, of course, picked up this phrase and used it to undermine Christianity and portray it as a hindrance to humanity's progress. Marx was really saying that man needs to forget about heaven altogether since it acts as an anaesthetic on his social conscience and prevents him from getting involved in the social injustices of the here and now.

It would be necessary to challenge Karl Marx on this, of course, since his conviction would not stand the scrutiny of historical fact. Some of those who have been in the forefront of social progress, and have vigorously challenged evil and pioneered social reform have believed most intensely in heaven. Lord Shaftesbury, for example, had printed at the top of his notepaper: 'Even so, come Lord Jesus'. He said in his biography: 'I do not think that in the last forty years I have lived one conscious hour that was not influenced by the thought of our Lord's return.' Heaven, far from being a drug, became a stimulant to vivify the social conscience and make our society fit for a King to return to.

The Church, however, has obviously through the years fallen for the twin jibes that heaven is either a delusion or a drug or both. Great and fearless Christian leaders like Martin Luther and John Calvin have little to say about heaven. Theologians give little space to the subject in their theological writing. Rheinhold Niebhur in *The Nature and Destiny of Man* has nothing on heaven and indeed the only reference he makes about it is one regrettable statement: 'It is unwise for Christians to claim any knowledge of either the furniture of heaven or the temperature of hell.'

What is the source, then, of our information about heaven? Amongst all the references to it in the Bible there are three first-hand witnesses who have been there, and an actual witness is always so much more convincing than someone who is only speculating. Most of what we know about heaven comes from these three. The apostle Paul tells of being caught up into Paradise where 'he heard inexpressible things, things that man is not permitted to tell'. The apostle John tells how he saw a door opened and he saw straight into heaven. Jesus, the Son of God, however, is our primary witness. He was there first before coming among us here on earth. He said: 'I have spoken to you of earthly things and you do not believe; how then will you believe if I speak of heavenly things? No one has ever gone into heaven except the one who came from heaven – the Son of Man.'

The language which all three use to convey their experience is naturally picture language and metaphor – how else could they communicate reality which is beyond man's experience? They answer three questions which most people would ask about heaven: 'Where is heaven?' 'What is it like?' 'Who will be there?'. Let's try to explore their answers!

First of all, *Where is heaven?* The difficulty in answering this question is that we cannot use the normal, human means for speaking of location in space. We cannot answer in geographical terms of latitude or longitude. We cannot answer in astronomical terms – even though man can probe eighty-two million light years into space with a radio telescope. This immediately stimulates a tendency to fantasy since we cannot locate heaven within the universe in geographical or astronomical terms. But although we are in a different dimension we are still in reality, for spiritual dimension is not discernible by our telescopes. When Thomas, one of Jesus' disciples, was concerned that he did not know how to get to heaven, Jesus simply told him not to be upset or confused or afraid. 'It is all right,' He said, 'I will take you there.' Jesus used an Eastern colloquialism for that; He said, 'I am the way.' In view of this I need not be too concerned since the only reason ultimately for wanting to locate a place is so that I might be able to find my way there. I would sense that although invisible to our mortal eyes and in a quite different dimension from the space/time concept which enables us to locate reality now on earth, heaven is much nearer than we think. However, as we are going to need new bodies to inhabit heaven, so we would need new eyes now to see it.

Heaven – the ultimate destination of the Christian – will include a new earth. The whole universe is going to be available to human beings in their resurrection bodies. This sounds fantastic, but it is nevertheless true. We are learning slowly that because a thing is thought to be, and talked about as, fantastic it does not cancel out its reality. For example, at the beginning of this century the enormous and incalculable power locked up in the atom would have sounded fantastic. We have come now however, not only to know, but to fear this reality. Again, if you had told the first Elizabethan age that one day they would be able to sit in their living room in Aberdeen and watch a football match in Göthenberg in Sweden, or switch on their television sets in

Glasgow and watch an opera live in London, or sit anywhere and watch men circling and landing on the moon – it would have sounded absurd. Today we regard it as part of the routine of life.

We should not be too surprised or sceptical that one day we will inhabit a new universe – renovated and spring-cleaned – because God says so! We know that this new heaven and new earth is going to have a metropolis – a capital city. Again there were days when that would have sounded absurd, but not now. We accept it as part of modern life that it is only a matter of time until there will be centres and colonies located in space. Man has only just arrived at this, but God thought of it first and has proceeded to do it. This metropolis will be fifteen hundred square miles according to the Bible.

One of the haunting questions which occurs to many when they think and speak of life after death is: 'If all these people in history come back to life for eternity, it is going to be pretty crowded is it not?' With confidence and expectancy we can answer: 'Not if we have a new universe to live in which is going to have a capital city of fifteen hundred square miles.' This latter could swallow up most of Europe as we know it today.

Where is heaven? That is not really the important question. The question that we really need to answer is 'How do I get there?' To that question Jesus answered quite unequivocally in a way which we can understand right now: 'I have gone to prepare a place for you. If this were not the case, I would have told you. One day I will come and get you, so do not be upset or afraid!' Often when I have had an appointment to keep somewhere this has brought peace to my heart. I am preparing at this time to go to Indonesia. I have never been there before. I fly from London to Hong Kong to Jakarta and there I am to meet Mr and Mrs Menayang, who will take me on the following day to Surabaya. Why should I worry about keeping my appointment in Surabaya, Mr and Mrs Menayang will make sure that I get there. I have a letter in my possession which says so!

The second question is just as pressing as the first: *What is it like?* Normally we find the answer to that question by being told the things which we can expect to see there and the things which will not be there. In heaven, for instance, there will be no churches, no temples, no religious buildings. This would normally be characteristic of any earthly community – the steeple; the dome; the spire; the minaret. These are the buildings which dominate the skyline. In London the dome of St Paul's Cathedral is as characteristic as the Post Office Tower or Big Ben or Tower Bridge. You see it and immediately identify London. It will not be so with heaven – God will be worshipped everywhere, and so buildings like that will be unnecessary.

There will be no sea in heaven. The sea, while intriguing man and giving him a great deal of pleasure, has been a threat as it has eroded his territory. It has also been an enemy as it has threatened his safety. It has also been a main cause of separation and division as it has created a geographical barrier between one race and another. The relationships which man will enjoy in heaven will not include sex. There will be love in the truest sense of each wanting the highest and best for the other and outdoing one another in honour – but sexual love will not be part of this. It is virtually impossible for us now to contemplate sexless relationships – yet even now as we experience the reality of the fellowship of the Holy Spirit in a tiny measure that possibility of a depth of satisfaction rarely found in this life becomes attractive beyond expression.

In heaven the surgeon, the doctor, the nurse, the pharmacist, the physiotherapist, the pathologist, the dentist, the dietician, the psychiatrist, will all be redundant, for there will be no suffering there. Pain will have gone, and physical, emotional and mental anxiety will have no place. In fact death will have gone forever, so the funeral director will be out of a job too! God gives assurance that there will be no sorrow or separation there either by death or distance. So there will be no weeping or mourning, because God is going to wipe away all the tears from our eyes. There will be light everywhere although the sun and the moon will be obsolete. God is light and His light will be there. Often it is in the darkness that pain and sorrow reach their height – but in heaven there will be no darkness at all.

Unity at last will be complete in heaven – there will be no racial, political, ecclesiastical, social, material, sexual, or economic segregation. All will be one. Rita Snowden has a wonderfully beautiful story. A new church was built. It was to be called 'the Church of the Christ-child'. The people who were planning it wanted a stained glass window to dramatise and summarise the love of Christ for the children. The theme of the window was to be:

Around the throne of God in Heaven
   Thousands of children stand
Children whose sins are all forgiven
   A holy, happy band,
Singing Glory! Glory! Glory!

They employed an artist to draw the picture for the window, and he produced a picture which he thought the best thing that he had ever done. When the picture was done he went to bed to sleep. He was wakened, as he thought, by a noise in the studio. He went into the studio and he found a stranger with a palette in his hand altering his picture. 'Stop!' he cried. 'You'll ruin it!' The stranger answered: 'You have already ruined it. You have five colours on your palette,' said the stranger, 'yet you have made the faces of all the children white. Who told you that all their faces were white in heaven?' 'No one told me, sir,' said the artist. 'I always thought of it that way.' The stranger said: 'You were wrong. I have simply used the colours you forgot to use, and made some of the faces yellow and some brown, and some black and some red. For these little ones have come from many, many lands in answer to my call.' 'Your call?' said the artist. 'What call was that, sir?' And the stranger's voice said: 'Suffer little children to come unto me.' There will be no segregation in heaven.

Nor will there be any sin there. We have come to settle for the fact that sin is a reality and so has to be put up with and handled as best we can. We accept it as normal, when in fact it is abnormal. God's normal, what God always intended should be, will be clearly seen in heaven. So accustomed are we to sin that we are unable to grasp a reality where there will be no temper tantrums or smouldering anger waiting to erupt like an uncontrollable volcano. There will be no lust or jealousy unleashed in destructive selfishness. There will be no gossip or back-biting ruining character and undermining confidence. There will be no corrosive resentment or bitterness which has so twisted and distorted life here on earth. The mind cannot grasp that this will be normal experience.

These are all things which are absent, but there are many other things which will be present. Heaven, for instance, will be a place of rest—not the armchair, king-size bed variety, but rest in the Biblical sense. In the Bible rest means freedom from mental and spiritual frustration. In fact it would appear to be a contradiction—but rest in the Bible seems to include busyness. There seem to be twenty-four hour shifts in heaven—but all to some significant purpose. There will be no frustration.

As we have already noticed there will be rewards in heaven—these will be given at the Judgment Seat of Christ. They have to do with our service here on earth and not with our salvation. Our salvation is secure on the basis of what God has already done for us in Christ on the Cross—but our service here on earth will be scrutinised in justice and rewarded accordingly. I do not fully understand this, but quite clearly the Bible teaches that our responsibility in heaven will be regulated by our response to the

107

opportunities, directions and resources of God to which we have responded here on earth.

Already we have thought negatively about there being no separation or segregation in heaven, but positively there will be perfect fellowship with nothing to mar it. God's desire is for fellowship, and in heaven it will be perfect. All through life the devil has partially achieved his object to isolate human beings one way or another, and all of us have felt the impact of his nefarious ministry. This will be finally and fully defeated.

Again, life on earth has been troubled by questions to which there seemed to be no satisfying answer and problems for which there appeared to be no adequate solution. Uncertainty, insecurity, confusion and anxiety have often resulted. But in heaven all of this will be swallowed up in revelation and light and truth and knowledge and understanding. The things which have been obscure will become plain, and worrying uncertainty will be gone forever.

The whole experience in heaven – which is quite beyond us to understand or appreciate – will be shot through with rejoicing. One of the first things we are going to have to do in heaven is to learn to sing a new song. There is more about singing in the Revelation of St John than in any other Book in the Bible apart from the Psalms. Handel's magnificent 'Hallelujah Chorus' which caused George II to stand and everyone else to stand ever since, comes from Revelation. All who go to heaven are going to be in the choir of heaven – even though they may be tone-deaf here on earth – since apparently one of the features of our new bodies will be the facility for unhindered praise.

We need to soak in the thrilling positives and the glorious negatives of heaven. To contemplate them is to create a deep desire to be part of them one day – and by the grace of God we will!

The third question which lurks not too far from the surface of our thinking is – *Who will be there?* Quite clearly

God will be there. It is His home. God is often spoken of by Christians as their Father in heaven or their heavenly Father. In fact when Jesus was responding to a request to teach His disciples to pray He taught them (and us!) to think clearly of their Father who is in heaven. It helps to create a very warm, domestic picture for us. However critical children may be of their home – for most there is nowhere quite like it. Death for the Christian is going home to be with Father.

The tombstone which marks the last earthly resting place of the founder of the Scouting movement, the former Chief Scout, Lord Baden-Powell, is very simple. It gives his name, date of birth and death and little else. However, it has a curious circle with a dot in the middle of it. This is a tracking sign which means 'gone home'. He taught boys to find their way through the countryside by means of signs which were left behind to guide them. The final sign was a circle with a dot in the middle which meant – if you want to find me now you will have to come to my home or to the camp. On every Christian grave there ought to be a circle with a dot in the middle! This is where God our Father lives – it is home!

Jesus will be there too! It is one of the realities of the Christian Gospel that there is already a man in heaven – Jesus. About six weeks after His crucifixion and resurrection – having appeared and disappeared to His disciples giving them Bible studies and preparing them to accept that He was just as real whether they could actually see Him or not – He eventually ascended to be with His Father in heaven. I sense that many parts of the Christian Church do not make as much of the Ascension as they ought. Jesus literally left earth – from the Mount of Olives near Jerusalem – with His disciples staring towards heaven as He ascended there in His new resurrection body. He is already there today! His work is certainly not ended, as Christians often sing, for He indicated that He wanted to go to heaven to prepare a place for us to live there too – in the new bodies

109

like His which one day we will possess. It is from heaven that Jesus will one day return to demonstrate His power and show His glory and judge both the living and the dead.

The *angels* will be there. We do not think too much about angels normally and give them little place in reality. Even most Christians would disregard them apart from the events of Christmas. From one December to the next Christians, along with non-Christians, would enter discussion on the question: 'Is there intelligent life elsewhere in the universe?' The Bible answered that question categorically two thousand years ago. The Bible speaks of angels in a matter-of-fact way – from Genesis to Revelation they are part of the story. Jesus told us what to think of them, for He had many dealings with them, and they quite obviously meant a great deal to Him. Dr Karl Barth once wrote: 'Where God is, there angels are. Where there are no angels there is no God.' If we do not believe in angels now, then immediately after death we surely will – for they will be there! We will spend life after death with them – either with the devil and his angels, or with God and His angels. One way or the other we will be with them – either the bad ones or the good ones.

One more category of being will be in heaven – human beings who are either perfect or have been pardoned. There has only been one perfect human being who ever lived on earth and He already is in heaven, so the remainder of human beings who get there will have to be the pardoned ones – those whose names are written in the Lamb's Book of Life. These are the ones who have trusted the provision of God in His Son Jesus Christ who died for their sin on the Cross on the hill of Calvary. They will be received into heaven, not on the basis of how hard they have tried to be good and do right, but on the basis of how simply they have trusted what God has already done for them in His Son Jesus Christ. We become God's children by our ears rather than by our hands. It is what we hear and so believe that matters rather than what we do. We can never earn our salvation or place in heaven, only receive it with a wondering and adoring heart.

God will have a huge family and it will take the whole of eternity to get to know the members of it. Fred Hoyle once said in a radio broadcast that he wanted three hundred years to live a full life and not just seventy or eighty years. But three hundred years would be woefully inadequate for all that God has in mind for us.

There are really only two destinies for men, and it is not necessary to choose between them. You only need to choose heaven since you need do nothing at all in order to go to hell. Notices which appear outside churches are often worse than useless because of their obscurity or platitudes, but one notice which I heard of arrested me: 'The road to hell – keep straight on. The road to heaven – right about turn.' In other words nobody ends up in heaven by accident, but many end up in hell that way, since the road there is paved with the good intentions that might have led in another direction had something been done about them.

How do you choose to go to heaven then? By trying to live a good life? By going to church? By getting baptised? By going to Communion? All of these things and many others have their place within a proper context, but none of them has the means to get us to heaven. There is only one way, and that is by trusting Jesus Christ, the Son of God, as your personal Lord and Saviour. One of Jesus' followers once displayed anxiety about how to get to heaven that many have subsequently shown. He knew Jesus was going to heaven and he wanted to know how to get there too. To his anxious enquiry Jesus responded: 'I am the way and the truth and the life. No one comes to the Father except through Me.' That is clear enough – and exclusive enough.

There is a verse in an old and well-loved hymn, written during the nineteenth century by Cecil Frances Alexander, that says it all:

He died that we might be forgiven,
  He died to make us good,
That we might go at last to heaven,
  Saved by His precious blood.

Christ has not promised His people a smooth passage, but only a safe landing.

8: Angels – This home has servants too!

We do not tend to give much thought or credence to the reality of angels – even those of us who are devoutly Christian. Angels very often in our thinking – if not in our speaking – are relegated to the realm of spiritual fairyland or the context of Santa Claus. Indeed for most of us Christmas is about the only time we give them consideration. We faithfully portray them on our Christmas cards; include them in our nativity plays; and refer to them in our Christmas carols. Well we might do this since the Christmas story in the Bible includes angels as an integral part. The angels are involved from the promise of a son, John the Baptist, to Zechariah, to the flight into Egypt to protect the baby Jesus. In between they make dramatic appearances to Mary, Joseph and the shepherds. But, Christmas over, they disappear for the rest of the year – even in the Church.

The Bible, however, does not promote such a careless or indifferent attitude to angels. From the Book of Genesis to the Book of Revelation angels are part of the unfolding story of man's redemption. It is difficult to see how we can be full Christians without belief in angels. Jesus certainly believed in angels – and He was never in the habit of speaking either in an accommodative sense or in expressing a superstitious belief existing among the Jews at that time. Jesus never failed to correct popular opinion and tradition when it was wrong.

Angels were present at Jesus' birth conducting the very delicate and sensitive negotiations whereby the Son of God would be born as a result of the ministry of the Holy Spirit co-operating with a human being. They were present, too, when the Spirit led Jesus into the wilderness to be confronted with the real implications of His incarnation – to challenge the rebellion of Satan with its catastrophic results. During the days of His ministry on earth Jesus was not alone – the angels were with Him. It was a constant source of encouragement to Him that the hosts of heaven were available although He did not call on their services. In the awesome darkness of the Garden of Gethsemene they did not forsake Jesus; in the eerie morning light of Easter day they were more surprised than the women who came to complete the embalming of Jesus' body and said with devastating logic – 'A cemetery is a place for dead people, so why would you come looking for someone who is alive here?' Underlying their directions they seemed to be saying: 'He is busy at the moment, but tell the disciples He will see them later!' On that unique day when He ascended from the Mount of Olives to heaven, having appeared and disappeared over six fantastic weeks to the disciples, the angels were there again giving directions to the disciples to go back to Jerusalem and wait until His promise would be fulfilled to send the Holy Spirit upon them.

Noticeably the only place where the angels were absent in the unfolding record of the Gospel is on the hill of Calvary. There Jesus was alone. This was the only crisis in Jesus' life where the angels were absent. It only increases the awfulness of that event – the sun had gone out; God had departed and forsaken His Son; the darkness that covered the earth was deep and impenetrable; and Jesus was alone! Such was the reality of His dealing with sin on our behalf. Well might Cecil Frances Alexander sing:

There was no other good enough
    To pay the price of sin;
He only could unlock the gate
    Of heaven, and let us in.

Until His birth the angels looked up to Jesus as the eternal Son of God. At His birth the angels looked down to Jesus, because the Son of God had become a baby on earth. Now Jesus is back sharing in the glory of His Father, and He is the Captain of the Lord's Hosts – the angels. There is a man in heaven today preparing a place for us – with the angels!

We need to confront the pictures which we have in our minds – if we think of them at all – about angels. Our understanding is often the result of traditional folklore, artistic licence or banal sentiment rather than the revelation of Scripture. A popular view of the angels is that they are incredibly beautiful creatures with bare feet and long white robes; with long blonde hair (always recently shampooed!) and clear blue eyes; with a circle of gold around their heads and a harp in their hands and the inevitable wings sprouting through their long cloaks from their shoulder blades. It would be difficult to mistake such a being were he to approach us and yet the Bible does indicate that sometimes we will entertain angels unawares. Abraham and Lot certainly did not know that they were dealing with a supernatural being when he appeared to them to deliver God's message. However perfect and attractive they may be we can be sure they are not as the artist has traditionally portrayed them.

Again, in the distress and pain of bereavement some have been comforted with the thought and belief that loved ones have not only gone to keep company with the heavenly host, but have them themselves become part of it. Again sentiment rather than Scripture has encouraged us. Angels and human beings are quite separate. It is true that even if we do not believe in angels on this side of the grave, we certainly will on the other side of the grave, since we will see the angels as they are, but there is no direct connection between human beings and angels. They are a different order of being and were created separately by a quite different process. Angels will never become men as such, nor will men become angels.

Perhaps the greatest fear among Christians is that if we give real credence to angels, in some way we will infringe the unique work of Jesus as the only Mediator (go-between) between man and God. This fear was heightened a few generations ago by a fad in England to dedicate church buildings to the saints and the angels. To call a church St Michael's was not unusual. Sometimes the practice was concerned to include the whole heavenly host, and so 'St Michael's and All Angels' was the name given to the building. However valid or confusing this practice was clearly the angels are neither to be worshipped nor prayed to. At least twice in the last Book of the New Testament the angels tell John who was given the vision by God. 'Do not fall down and worship me!', the angel was saying: 'I am just a servant of God as you are!' The angels are simply the servants of God who take His word to men and do whatever He tells them. We, as human beings, do not have any claim on them yet, but one day we will, and they will be the servants of Christians in heaven. In the meantime there is only one Mediator (go-between) between man and God and that is Jesus Christ. We go straight to God through Jesus Christ alone. So far as the angels are concerned the traffic flow, the direction they take, is from God to man and not vice versa.

The Bible, however, does say some positive things about the angels. They are a distinct order of being between God and man – although neither God nor man.

First the angels are superior to man in strength, beauty and intelligence. They do not get born as man does and subsequently grow up, marry and have children. Their number is fixed by God who made them. God created them as He wanted them to be. They do not have bodies as we have (although apparently they have the power to appear as men) and so they do not die as we do. They belong to heaven rather than earth.

Secondly they are inferior to God. Although vastly superior to men they do not share God's power nor His knowledge. They are not eternal as God is eternal – there was a time when they were not and had to be created.

Thirdly although only a few angels are named in Scripture (e.g. Michael, Gabriel and Lucifer) they are quite clearly countless in number. The Bible speaks of them as being ten thousand times ten thousand and myriads upon myriads. Although there are titles, ranks and grades among the angels (e.g. archangels, cherubims, seraphims, principalities and powers) and their number is fixed, it appears to be a vast number. In the Hebrew language the word which is used to describe the biggest possible number is the word 'host' – and this word is used of the angels.

Fourthly the Bible speaks of their beauty as astounding. Were we to see them in their proper milieu of heavenly glory we would acknowledge their utter beauty, splendour and magnificence. Throughout the history of art, sculptors and painters have been intrigued by and attracted to the human form. But so far they have been unable to encapsulate the magnificent beauty of the angels by artistic form.

Fifthly the angels have unusual strength so far as human beings are concerned. There is the remarkable Old Testament record of how Jacob wrestled with an angel one night and came off second best in the encounter and ended up by being lame for the rest of his life. One of the prophets tells us that 186,000 foot-soldiers are no match for one angel. The desolation of Sodom and Gomorrah is the result of two angels' activities. So we are not dealing with innocuous, irrelevant beings who appear beatific, sing songs and blow trumpets.

Sixthly although they are not omniscient like God they are far more intelligent than men are. They know, for example, what is going on in our lives and what is happening throughout the earth. They are more informed than anyone on earth is. In a quite specific way the Bible tells us, however, that although the angels have great intelligence and understanding they do not know the time when Jesus Christ will return to earth.

117

Seventhly they have remarkable speed. God's servant Daniel prayed one night in his need and God despatched an angel to assist him. If you read Daniel's prayer aloud (Daniel 9) it would take only a minute or so – but the angel was there in his bedroom before he had finished praying.

The *final* thing that the Bible says about the angels is that there are not only good angels, but bad ones as well. Perhaps this is the most important thing that is revealed about the angels. One third of the angels decided to rebel against God and try to take His Kingdom from Him, and so there is strife not only on earth, but in the heavenly places too. Much of the pain and heartache we experience on earth is simply an outcrop of this heavenly conflict. God will deal with it finally one day and there will not only be a new earth, but a new heaven as well.

Man has succeeded in putting men on the moon and constructing a space craft which can orbit the earth and return with almost unbelievable accuracy only to be sent out on its mission once more. Man is pushing the frontiers of space back gradually by manned space flight and by other means. As man's attention is increasingly turned outwards, he inevitably asks the question, 'Is there intelligent life elsewhere in the universe?' The Bible affirmed that long ago in its revelation when it indicated quite clearly that the angels are real.

As the messengers of God to men they are concerned for little children and they rejoice over men and women who repent and believe that Jesus Christ is Lord and so enter the Kingdom of God. They surround those who are in dangerous situations and have fearful hearts. Jacob was homesick on his first night away from home, but the angels were there. Elisha was completely surrounded by the enemy in Dothan and his young servant was terrified. He cried out to God to let this young man see what the real situation was and his servant saw clearly that between the Syrians and Elisha there was another ring of God's chariots. With wonder in his heart he saw the angels touch the eyes of the

Syrians as they advanced towards Elisha and complete confusion resulted. Daniel was thrown to the lions, but the angels kept their savage and hungry mouths tight shut. The angels cooked meals for at least two people in the wilderness according to the Old Testament – for Hagar and for Elijah. They are the messengers of judgment and punishment as a man and his wife discovered when the Garden of Eden was barred to them by an angel as a result of their disobedience; as the inhabitants of Sodom and Gomorrah discovered; as the infantry of the Assyrians discovered when they besieged Jerusalem. In the New Testament Peter is released from prison by an angel; Paul is comforted during a dangerous sea voyage by an angel – and so on and on.

It is not possible to believe that the Bible is true and accurate and not believe in angels. But their service to man continues to the present day. There are some remarkable incidents told about angelic help in much more modern times. Some of these are well known and well documented. For example, towards the end of August, 1914, though the British Army was outnumbered three to one and on the verge of annihilation by the advancing Germans at Mons, a heavenly host intervened between the rival armies, saving the British and causing the enemy to flee in panic. The German forces, after sweeping all resistance aside, had advanced on a wide front into the heart of Belgium and France. Although the Belgians, French and British put up a strong resistance, it was principally against the British that the heaviest enemy attacks were launched. The British troops, greatly outnumbered, had been fighting continuously for several days, with little or no rest and were greatly fatigued. The prolonged rearguard action had lost considerable numbers of men and guns. Serious defeat appeared to be inevitable, especially as no reserves seemed to be forthcoming. It began to dawn on the British Army that a 'Day of Trouble' had arrived and that God alone could help and save. In Britain people were called to prayer, and the churches were crowded for prayer throughout the nation. It was then that the event, afterwards known as the appearance of the 'Angels of Mons', occurred in answer to national prayer. Of several accounts referring to the appearance of the angels, the following two are typical, both having been related by British soldiers who vouched for the occurrences as having been observed by them personally.

' 'While a detachment of British soldiers was retiring through very heavy German artillery and machine-gun fire in August, 1914, they knelt behind a hastily erected barricade and endeavoured to hold up the enemy advance. The firing on both sides was very intensive, and the air reverberated with deafening clashes of exploding shells.

Suddenly, firing on both sides stopped dead and a silence fell. Looking over their barrier, the astonished British saw four or five wonderful beings much bigger than men, between themselves and the halted Germans. They were white-robed and bare-headed, and seemed rather to float than stand. Their backs were towards the British, and they faced the enemy with outstretched arm and hand, as if to say: "Stop, thus far and no further." The sun was shining quite brightly at the time. The next thing the British knew was that the Germans were retreating in great disorder.'

On another occasion, the British were in danger of being surrounded by the Germans, and had lost numbers of guns and men. Just when matters seemed hopeless, the heavy enemy fire suddenly stopped dead and a great silence fell over all.

'The sky opened with a bright shining light and figures of "luminous beings" appeared. They seemed to float between the British and German forces, and to prevent the further advance of the enemy. Some of the German cavalry were advancing and the officers and men were unable to get their horses to go forward.

Before the surprised British were able to realise what had happened, the whole of the apparently victorious enemy force was retreating in great disorder. This allowed the British and the Allied Armies to re-form and fall back upon a line of defence several miles further west, where they "dug in".'

Some years later the 'Angels of Mons' were remembered. During that same war in 1918 the whole British nation was called to prayer, and the President of the United States of America did likewise. So there was united prayer from all over the English-speaking world. A German officer gave the following account of events as they were shared with his lieutenant:

'Herr Kapitan, just look at that open ground behind Bethune. There is a brigade of cavalry coming up through the smoke drifting across it. They must be mad, these English, to advance against such a force as ours in the open. I suppose they must be cavalry of one of their Colonial forces, for see, they are all in white uniform and are mounted on white horses.

"Strange," I said, "I never heard of the English having any white-uniformed cavalry, whether Colonial or not. They have all been fighting on foot for several years past, and anyway, they wear khaki, not white."

"Well, they are plain enough," he replied. "See, our guns have got their range now; they will be blown to pieces in no time."

We saw the shells bursting amongst the horses and their riders, all of whom came forward at a quiet walk trot, in parade ground formation, each man and horse in his exact place.

Shortly afterwards, our machine guns opened a heavy fire, raking the advancing cavalry with a dense hail of lead. But they came quietly forward, though the shells were bursting amongst them with intensified fury, and not a single man or horse fell.

Steadily they advanced, clear in the shining sunlight; and a few paces in front of them rode their leader – a fine figure of a man, whose hair, like spun gold, shone in an aura round his bare head. By his side was a great sword, but his hands lay quietly holding his horse's reins, as his huge

121

white charger bore him proudly forward.

In spite of heavy shell, and concentrated machine-gun fire, the White Cavalry advanced, remorseless as fate, like the incoming tide surging over a sandy beach. Then a great fear fell on me, and I turned to flee; yet I, an Officer of the Prussian Guard, fled, panic-stricken, and around me were hundreds of terrified men, whimpering like children, throwing away their arms and accoutrements in order not to have their movements impeded . . . all running. Their intense desire was to get away from that advancing White Cavalry; but most of all from their awe-inspiring Leader.

That is all I have to tell you. We are beaten. The German Army is broken. There may be fighting, but we have lost the war. We are beaten – by the White Cavalry . . . I cannot understand.'

Many prisoners were examined and questioned, and in substance, their accounts tallied with the one given here. All this in spite of the fact that it is known that no cavalry was deployed in action either there or elsewhere at that particular time. This led to a great advance in this sector between Bethune and Ypres during the ensuing weeks of July, 1918. Official reports tell us that between the 11th July, when the Allied advance began and the Armistice which ended the war on the 11th November at 11 am, the British and Allied forces captured 385,000 prisoners and over 5,000 guns.

From time to time in these days a similar testimony emerges, often not so spectacular, but sometimes more so. We are not only talking of the past, but also of the present and the future, for we are talking of reality.

The Bible tells us that Lazarus was carried by angels to Abraham's bosom. The angels, then, will serve us when we get to heaven – showing us around, and taking us to where we need to be. In a spectacular way they will accompany Jesus on His triumphant return to earth at the end of history as we know it. If we do not believe in angels now, and we dismiss some accounts of their present activity, the day is coming when our doubts will be dispelled.

We need to notice, however, that there are not only good angels, but, at this time, bad angels in the heavenly realm. At present these are not yet in some underworld, but there in the heavenlies. This answers one of the most insistent and deepest questions that confront us: 'Where did evil come from?' There is not much in the Bible about how evil began with the angels, but we do know that the real battle between darkness and light, between sin and righteousness, between good and evil, is in heaven and not on earth. These angels of darkness (or demons) are trying to deceive and delude men, to destroy and disintegrate the personalities of men.

Their leader is Satan, and his aim is to be God. He rebelled against God and took one third of the angels with him. He wants to have a kingdom of his own. Not only do men and women have free will before God, but so also do the angels. They were created to be messengers and not machines, and so they have the ability to say, 'No!' as well as the ability to say, 'Yes!' to God. So evil did not originate with God nor with man, but with the angels.

It is inevitable that as soon as our Christianity becomes supernatural (which is normal Christianity) and we break through in reality into heavenly places, and the Holy Spirit is operating effectively and relevantly in our lives, then the organised hierarchy of evil will also become real and significant to us. The dedicated task of the hosts of wickedness is to oppose and hinder the work of God and so stop the Kingdom of God from being extended.

So the universe at this time is in a permanent state of war. Whether the nation we live in is at peace or at war, every Christian within it is at war – not against people or social evils (although these may well be the manifestations of the real conflict!), but against 'beings without human bodies'. This is why Christians are called not only to be the sons of God and the servants of God, but also to be the soldiers of God. This is why the Church is intended to be not only a hospital for the sick, but a barracks for soldiers. We are involved in spiritual warfare as well as a spiritual walk. When we really became Christians something revolutionary and supernatural happened and we were put into a supernatural dimension of life–into a heavenly realm where there is war!

This is why we cannot stop the strife, the carnage, and the wars and fighting within the human race–we never really deal with the real enemy. The real enemy is not the one which is seen, but one which is unseen by our human eyes.

This is the reason too for the tumultuous inner conflicts which disturb and often distress us deeply–we are in a battle! Christians are often puzzled and sometimes despair over this phenomenon until they realise that the real conflict is in heaven and the conflicts within and among the nations and the human heart are the outcrop of the conflicts in heaven.

This is why Jesus taught His disciples to pray: 'Give us this day our daily bread'–we need to come quickly to an understanding of how utterly dependent we are daily on the provision of God to keep our bodies functioning!

'Forgive us our debts, as we forgive our debtors'–we need to come quickly to an understanding that Satan is a legalist and he is on the prowl to find victims whom he can devour. The main loopholes which we give him are when we choose to do wrong rather than right; when we have an unforgiving heart towards another; and when we dabble in occult practices in its variety of expressions.

'Lead us not into temptation, but deliver us from the evil one'–we need to come quickly to an understanding of who our real enemy is and there is never a minute when we need to be under his evil power. We can resist him in the strong name of Jesus Christ, the Son of God who died on the Cross for us, thereby stripping the bad angels of their power in the universe.

One day the devil and his angels will be moved from

heaven to earth and ultimately be banished to hell! Then they will never again be able to trouble the creatures God has redeemed. They will be held in God's detention block forever. God will create a new heaven and a new earth having 'spring-cleaned' the old heaven and the old earth. He will make all things new – where heaven and earth will be freed from every trace of evil.

Our future will contain angels! Our choice is with what angels will we spend it – with the devil and his angels in hell, or with God and His angels in heaven?

9: There are so many questions

Because of the nature of death, because of our human limitation to grasp that reality, and because of the profound personal and emotional involvement so often it is difficult not to have questions which are burning and urgent within us. Over the years many of these questions have been asked in a highly charged emotional and personal context. I would like to select a few which are constantly recurring in one form or another, and 'scramble' them so as to avoid any personal identification.

Question 1

I am learning to accept that Ted will never come in for tea again, but often during these past months I feel he is looking down on us approving or disapproving of the things we are doing. I often wish I could turn to him to ask him what he thinks, and what I should do. At other times it is as if his spirit is still here although his body is not. Is it wrong to feel this way? Does it really show lack of faith in God?

I can think of nothing more natural and inevitable than that where there has been an intimate and warm relationship between two human beings and suddenly it is ended by death that the desire to maintain it remains. There will be a certain momentum which will continue after the event of death. Normally the practical implications of this will diminish with the passage of time. Guilt, however, should not lie heavily upon us over something which is natural if not even inevitable. The time of adjustment will vary as circumstances are always different in every case – it is quite impossible to generalise!

There are some subtle dangers, however, that need to be carefully noticed and guarded against. The Bible does speak about 'a great crowd of witnesses' in the grandstands of heaven who surround us. There is some ambiguity as to whether they are looking at us or at Jesus. There is also some ambiguity as to whether they are to provide inspiration for us or to make intercession for us. If the latter then it is only a short step for us to make prayers to the dead and to the saints to help us. However strongly some Christian traditions would allow this there is certainly no clear Biblical encouragement to do it. The strong Biblical note is on the communion of saints. This appears to find its expression in Christ rather than in one another.

Again it will stifle life if we live it in order to please someone who is dead. I can remember a little boy who was tragically drowned trying to rescue his dog. For years his parents behaved as if he were still alive and organised their holidays and maintained his bedroom in exactly the same way as they had done during his lifetime. In fact his bedroom was kept exactly as he had left it on the day he died. It reminded me of the Charles Dickens character Miss Havisham in *Great Expectations*. She is shown as a pathetic, dehumanised figure who ruined her life by her unwillingness and refusal to face heartbreak. As a young woman she had been swept off her feet by a whirlwind romance. Marriage plans were made; the date for the wedding was decided; the wedding dresses were bought; and the wedding feast prepared.

At 8.40 am on the morning of the wedding, the bridegroom's letter had come, cancelling the marriage. Miss Havisham refused to accept the truth. She pronounced a curse on her lover and tried to make time stand still. All the clocks in the house were stopped at twenty minutes to nine. The curtains were drawn so that the world outside could never remind her of the passing hours or the changing seasons. The wedding feast lay mouldering on the table. As the years passed all that happened was that she became an embittered and eccentric old lady in a faded wedding gown. Although this is extreme in its detail and bizarre in its outworking, nevertheless it is almost a parable of some lives which mentally if not physically stifle the reality of life in the same way. That is unhealthy and quite clearly never what God intended.

To feel that Ted's spirit is still present on earth is a contradiction of the Bible's clear teaching. His memory and influence may remain – but not his spirit. As we have already noticed, at death body and spirit are separated. Our spirits go to God direct, whereas our bodies go to the grave. In the case of Jesus' death His Spirit was commended to God and His body was given to Joseph of Arimathea to care for. We have seen that there is a day coming when body and spirit will be reunited, but at death they are separated. This is what death really involves.

God, of course, is quite capable of responding to our requests for wisdom and guidance to face up to the real issues of life and find a proper way (in fact, His way) through them. We may not always be adept at receiving His guidance clearly, but this does not indicate His unwillingness to give it. It is only as we constantly look to Him that we will become more and more able to appreciate the desires of His heart. God knows every detail of our situation, including the bereftness which we feel in the loss of a loved one. I believe that in the midst of grief He desires very specially to help us and to guide the direction of our life.

These are dangers which need to be guarded against, but there needs to be one final, strong note of warning – communication with the dead is forbidden by God (e.g. Deuteronomy 18:11; Isaiah 8:19, 20). The consequences of disregarding this prohibition are real, far-reaching, and have a profound practical implication for the worse for the person who does.

Question 2

Will we be able to recognise one another in heaven—especially if disease, accident or age has changed our bodily form in life?

Jesus was certainly changed after His resurrection and yet clearly His identity remained. For a period of six weeks He kept appearing and disappearing to many—on one occasion to five hundred people at one time. Sometimes He came after His death and resurrection to individuals and sometimes to groups, but always with recognition. So He prepared them for the time He would ascend to His Father in Heaven and when they would no longer be able to see Him with their physical eyes. But as on earth after His resurrection so also He will be in heaven—recognisable! This reality convinced even a Thomas! As with Jesus, so with us. Jesus during His earthly ministry and before His death spent a great deal of His time convincing men and women of His spiritual qualities. After His resurrection—in those few short, precious weeks—He spent a great deal of His time convincing them of His 'physical' qualities. He seemed to be saying constantly—at least to everyone apart from Mary in the Garden of Gethsemane—look at Me; touch Me; feel Me; watch Me eating—it is really Me; I am real: I am the same person who lived with you; ate with you; taught you; showed you how to do things; laughed with you; cried with you.

The Bible clearly associates our resurrection as Christians with Jesus' resurrection—as it is with Him so it will be with us. In that marvellous chapter in the Bible on the resurrection body (1 Corinthians 15) the Holy Spirit instructs us:

> . . . the truth is that Christ has been raised from death, as the guarantee that those who sleep in death will also be raised . . . each one will be raised in his proper order: Christ, first of all; then, at the time of His coming, those who belong to Him.

So as He was changed, yet unchanged; glorified, yet recognisable; so will we be.

On the mountain where Jesus went with three of His disciples and He was transfigured (whatever that means!) they quite clearly saw two of God's great servants of the past – Moses and Elijah. They spoke to Him of His God-given task of being Redeemer of the world. The experience was accompanied by God's affirmation of who Jesus was. But two figures from the past of centuries before were not only clearly alive, but recognisable to all who were present on that day. It is difficult to know how this recognition came in view of all that the Bible teaches about the past event of the death experience, but obviously it came clearly enough to convince them and impress them.

In a more general way we would recognise our imperfection here and now – our faculties are impaired by the fall of man and the sin of our own hearts. This affects every part of us. When we see Jesus Christ we are going to be perfected and made complete, and so presumably our understanding and appreciation of reality will be greater at that time rather than lesser. Paul, writing to those same Corinthians, says:

> What I know now is only partial; then it will be complete – as complete as God's knowledge of me.

Not only will we have a better understanding of God, but also a better understanding of one another.

In a less persuasive way, and yet nevertheless significant, wherever there has been a conviction that there is life after death there has often been a conviction that there would be some kind of recognition in that future life. Deep within the human personality is this desire for personal identity – God does not put these things within us to mock us! After all, if He writes our names in the Lamb's Book of Life, presumably one day He would want to put a face to the name!

If there is an 'interval' between death and resurrection
– before we enter heaven – does this give grounds for
believing in Purgatory?

The Bible does give grounds for believing in Purgatory –
but it occurs in *this* life not in the *next*. Jesus taught, on the
night before He died when He shared many things with His
disciples in the Upper Room and also on the journey from
it to the Garden of Gethsemane, that God purges Christians
in order that their lives would be relevant and productive.
The figure He used was that of the gardener pruning the
branches of the vine (John 15:1–17). There are some
branches which do not produce fruit, but only leaves.
There are other branches which produce fruit, but that fruit
is small and hard and sour. So the gardener either removes
or revitalises the vine by pruning (or purging) the branches.
In December and February sometimes the gardener will
'cut back' or prune or purge his vines until they look as if
they are dead. Sometimes God finds it necessary to do that
with us. In fact for most of us it is always necessary. The
main means that God uses to purge us is by using His
Word.

However there is no trace in the Bible of a place of
punishment *after* death where we pay for our sins which
have not been confessed and forgiven *before* death and
where we are cleansed and purged until we become saintly
enough to enter heaven. Alongside the view of Purgatory
being post-death is the concept that there are two categories
of people who die 'in faith'. The first category are those
who are regarded as perfect when they die, and they are
subsequently canonised and actually called saints. The
other category comprises of a very much larger number –
the majority in fact – who are not ready for heaven and so
have to be purged. In actual fact there was only one person
completely perfect at His death, and that was Jesus. Everyone else has to come into the imperfect category. This belief

131

in Purgatory has given rise to a whole range of practices which have often stained the history of the Church.

We cannot accept this view, however, because of some very clear Bible teaching.

Firstly, Jesus was punished on the Cross for *all* my sins — past, present, and future. Nothing has been left untouched or undealt with. It would be unjust to demand further punishment for that which has been so completely punished before.

Secondly, when I die physically I am set free from the bridgehead which sin has used — my body. I am no longer a target or a victim for Satan, temptation or sin. A corpse is unresponsive to temptation no matter how subtle or strong.

Thirdly, there are categorical statements from God that when Jesus appears in order to wind up history as we know it, and to bring everything to a satisfactory conclusion, believers in Him will become like Him — in a moment, in the twinkling of an eye, and we shall be changed. So there is no need either for a place or for a period of cleansing after death.

Question 4

To make this life on earth the final place of decision over where we should spend eternity seems very drastic. Will there never be another opportunity to respond to God's grace? There are parts of the Bible which seem to suggest that there will be.

The overwhelming evidence of the Bible is that in this life we determine our destiny according to how we respond to God as we have had opportunity to know Him. Some have not had the opportunity of knowing the reality of forgiveness since they have not had the chance to hear the Gospel of the Lord Jesus Christ. But all have some knowledge of God through the world of creation around them or the reality of conscience within them. Both of these factors in life have given all men a knowledge of God. God will deal with us then according to how we have recognised Him and responded to Him now. Man throughout the world in every generation has consistently not lived according to the light he has received – however limited that may have been and however imperfectly he may have perceived it. Man has never been totally innocent before God, but guilty. This is why it is so essential to share the Good News of Jesus Christ with all men – not to make them guilty, but to give them the peace of a forgiven heart.

Beyond the grave there is not one destiny, but two, since we are not all going to the same place, but one of two different places – heaven or hell. There is no need to make any decision in this life about the latter in order to arrive there, but we need to make a clear choice if we hope to experience the former. What we do before death will be absolutely decisive in determining what we will be doing after death. Such is the clear urgency in the Bible to take God seriously, ourselves seriously, and eternity seriously *now!*

The passage in which it is alleged that there is teaching about 'a second chance of salvation' is in Peter's First Letter, in the third chapter and verses 18 to 20:

> For Christ died for sins once for all, the righteous for
> the unrighteous, to bring you to God. He was put to
> death in the body, but made alive by the Spirit,
> through whom also He went and preached to the spirits
> in prison who disobeyed long ago while God waited
> patiently in the days of Noah while the ark was being
> built.

Whatever the implications of such a passage it does seem a very strange human reaction to 'dice with death' for the sake of argument, when there is so much evidence to encourage and even warn us that we need to settle eternal issues now. It is always dangerous to search around in the Bible for some part which will support our argument We are not trying to win arguments on an issue like this, but rather to secure eternal salvation. The passage from Peter's First Letter in any case seems to relate to the special circumstances of those who were prematurely judged by God and drowned in the days of Noah. Our circumstances are quite different, and we have the opportunity to settle our eternal destiny rationally and securely now.

Question 5

Is it right to think that those who die are with Jesus immediately? The Bible seems to indicate that the dead are in a 'resting place' and remain there until Jesus returns. That 'resting place' or Gehenna seems such an unfriendly place and unattractive to us here on earth – what are people doing there? There are indications that dead people can be contacted through mediums, so surely they are not with Christ at that point? Can you say anything about this?

The *first* thing which I want to say is that there is no doubt at all from the Bible that those who have died as Christians (really knowing what it means to be born again by the Spirit and having lived realising that the desire of God is that we should live aware that Jesus is not only our Saviour, but also our Lord) will immediately be in the presence of Jesus. The most persuasive evidence for this is that Jesus told one of the thieves who died alongside Him on another cross that on that very day he would be with Him in Paradise. This is a categorical statement. The apostle Paul also clearly teaches, under the direction of the Holy Spirit, that to be absent from the body (i.e. his spirit has separated from his body in death) is to be present with the Lord. He also expresses the deep longing of his heart, as an apostle, to depart and so to be with Christ. Paul has arrived at a point where he no longer wants to stay on earth, but is willing to go to heaven, but rather now is willing to stay on earth, but really wants to go to heaven. The great, magnetic attraction for him is not only that all the pressure and responsibility and pain of this life will be over, but also that he will be able to enjoy the presence of Christ.

Secondly, there is no doubt that there is an 'interval' between death and resurrection. This is a time when our disembodied spirits dwell in Sheol or Hades (the place of departed spirits). This is not our permanent destination, but a resting place until Jesus returns to earth in power and glory, and we will then be resurrected for judgment. It is impossible to be precise about what people will be doing during this period. All that we know is that those who have died 'in Christ' will be in Paradise or the Garden of God. What will occupy people in such a place? Those who have not died 'in Christ' will be in Prison – not 'hell', but the prison part of Hades or Sheol. What will occupy people in such a place?

Thirdly, we need to be careful about the words we use for the immediate experience of life after dying. There has been a great deal of imprecision and so confusion here. Gehenna is different from Sheol or Hades. Gehenna is the final abode of the damned. It is the word which Jesus used for Hell. It is a post-resurrection destination for those who have been resurrected to condemnation. Heaven, too, is different from either Sheol or Hades. It is the post-resurrection destination for those who have been resurrected to salvation. It is the place which Jesus is preparing now for those who love Him – and a place is a location where bodies can dwell.

The sequence of events then is life on earth; death and the separating of body and spirit; the interval between death and final resurrection with our new eternal bodies; resurrection when Jesus has returned in power and glory to earth; judgment either for salvation or service; then either heaven or hell for eternity.

Fourthly, we need to notice clearly again that the practice of contacting the spirits of the dead is not only dangerous for us in this life, but also very deceptive – so that what we

135

think we have touched of reality is not real at all.

Question 6

God created man in His own image, and He was pleased with what He had made. Yet He allowed Satan to be in a position where he could spoil it all. Why did God allow this, how can we be sure that this will not happen again when God creates a new heaven and a new earth? Surely what happened once can happen again?

We need to answer the question first of all: 'Why did God allow Satan to spoil what is good?' The answer to that question is that when God created beings – both angelic and human – He created them with freedom of choice, with free will. So spiritual beings – as human beings – have the ability to accept or reject Him; submit to Him or rebel against Him; to say yes or no to Him; acknowledge Him or disregard Him. Although this whole area is difficult for us to understand we can appreciate that God did not create robots or machines when He created beings – both with and without human bodies. We can understand that love is not love unless it is freely given, and God, who is love, created beings in His own image to love Him. So apparently freedom of choice was necessary to enable them to respond in this way. There was a whole group of spiritual beings or angels who chose not to respond to God, but to reject Him – this group was led by Satan.

The second question we need to answer is: 'How can we be sure that this will not happen again?' The answer to that question is that there is a very clear procedure set out in the Bible about how God will deal with Satan. The Bible indicates that there are a number of judgments ahead – not just one. For example the Christians will be judged before the Judgment Seat of Christ – this will be for an evaluation of their service and not a condemnation of their sin (that has already been dealt with by Jesus on His Cross). The living nations will be judged by God, and separately, Israel will be judged by God. Those who have rejected Jesus Christ and those who have not lived according to the light and understanding they have received will be judged at what is called the Great White Throne – it will be a judgment of sin which will take place there. The rebellious or fallen angels will also be judged separately.

The Bible quite categorically says that Satan is under a perpetual curse, and that there is no removal of that curse. He is finally to be cast alive into the lake of fire, there to be tormented and controlled for ever. Those who have responded to his blandishments will accompany him. It was left to Jesus by God to say this clearly:

> Then I will turn to those on my left and say, 'Away with you, you cursed ones, into the eternal fire prepared for the devil and his demons.'

It all adds up to a picture of absolute control of evil for ever.

When you add, on the positive side, all that God has promised and revealed about heaven it is quite clear that the intrusion of evil to spoil things will never occur again. There are some quite remarkable things God has said about heaven.

In heaven there will be love without passion for we shall be like Jesus Christ. There will be service without weariness because His servants shall serve Him for ever. There will be holiness without imperfection because His Name will be in our foreheads. There will be blessing without curse because there will be no more curse. There will be life without death for there will be no more death. There will be joy without sorrow for God will wipe away all tears from our eyes. There will be light without darkness for there will be no night there. There will be glory without suffering because there will be no more pain. There will be singing without crying for there will be no more crying. There will be satisfaction without want because hunger and thirst will cease. There will be rule without end for we will reign with Him for ever. There will be beauty without infirmity because we will be without spot or wrinkle. There will be living without sinning because we will be faultless before God. There will be presence without absence for we will be forever with the Lord.

There is so much which is positive and new in heaven — so many concrete assurances given — that it will not be possible for there to be a repeat of the failure of us to be what God always intended us to become.

Question 7

What can I do about a loved one whom I know must ultimately go to hell?

I presume that in the mind of the questioner the loved one has died and is awaiting resurrection. In this case the brief answer to that question is 'nothing'! However there are comments that need to be made. We can never really know what has gone on in a person's heart, either prior to death or at the point when death was occurring, between God and himself. It is always a possibility that someone did respond to Jesus Christ without our knowing anything about it. The expression of the reality of that life is not always according to our particular traditions or preconceived ideas. The criteria for our dismissing a person as not being a Christian are not always Biblical or accurate. Sometimes our concern for them is because they do not do the things we think they should do nor do they refrain from doing the things that we think they should not do.

Again we need to be absolutely assured that God will do what is right and fair by our loved ones. So far as God is concerned there will be no mistakes or miscarriages of justice. He knows everything and so there will be perfect judgment. This is very difficult for us to conceive.

For the present, however, it makes it all the more

important that we should be vitally concerned about our loved ones before they die. We have a responsibility to share the reality of the Gospel with them even though that might cause awkwardness and even embarrassment. Often the reason for our awkwardness is that there is insufficient evidence in our own lives that there has been a revolutionary change and we are living in the new dimension of the Spirit. God's intention for us is that we should be living naturally supernatural lives. Our task is not to be rude or offensive, but natural. The quality of our life ought to demand that we give some explanation for it – and that explanation can only be given in terms of the reality of Christ and the fullness of the Holy Spirit.

There are so many questions and so many answers to them. Some of these questions about death are purely academic, but others are deeply personal and terribly urgent. At best we find ourselves limited in our answering since we have such an imperfect appreciation of life far less death. There will always be an air of mystery around the latter until we experience its reality for ourselves. However the important issue is not to answer every question or solve every problem, but to resolve to spend the rest of our lives in such a way that we will face the event of death without shame or regret. As you read now you are aware that this is the beginning of the rest of your life. You may find it helpful, if you are uncertain about your eternal destiny, to use this prayer:

Lord Jesus, I repent of my sin and come to you now for forgiveness and cleansing. I believe that you are the Son of God and that you died for my sins. Thank you for forgiving my sins. Thank you for the knowledge of life after death. Thank you for letting me know how important I am to you.

Lord Jesus, I want now to spend what remains of my life fulfilling your purposes and doing your will. I want to be completely freed from any area of darkness where

139

your light and your life has not fully penetrated. I want
to live my life as an obvious citizen of the Kingdom of
God and to be an effective and relevant part of the
Body of Christ. I will turn away from all wrongdoing,
and I will avoid everything that leads to wrongdoing.
I offer my life to you, and with your help and
guidance, I will obey you as my Lord. I ask you now
to baptise me in the Holy Spirit, and to release me in
praise in a way I have never praised you before.

10: Bereavement – Please, may I have permission to cry?

Death is one of those peculiar phenomena which always seems to happen to someone else and never to us. We touch it – often vaguely and academically – in the lives of others as spectators with a varying degree of interest. But approximately two-thirds of a million people die in Britain alone each year. That means that two-thirds of a million families are affected to some greater or lesser degree each year by the presence of death. There is an inevitability that one year we will be included as a statistic. How people cope will depend on a large number of factors. Bereavement will take many forms and cannot be approached by some standard formula either personally or professionally. The elderly lady whose husband dies peacefully after a very full and satisfying life will have very different needs from the young woman whose husband dies at the age of 40, leaving her with three young children to bring up. The parents who suffer the tragic loss of their young child in an accident will have very different needs from the single lady whose elderly mother, with whom she lived and looked after with devotion and love, eventually dies after some years of increasing physical discomfort and mental decline. The husband who returns home after the day's work to find his wife lying dead on the floor will have very different needs from the teenager who watches her father decline and decay before her eyes day by day with some terminal illness.

How we cope with bereavement – or don't cope with it – will depend upon a large number of factors, including the circumstances in which death occurred, the personal faith which we have, the support offered to us by doctors, ministers, friends, family etc., our own feelings about the deceased, how our loved one died and so on and on.

Each grief is individual and awfully personal. However well-intentioned and kind and genuine it may be, the person who says: 'I know *just* how you feel!' is off target. The bereaved person deep within him will instinctively react: 'No, you don't!' This is the very nature of bereavement. Every agony is a new and private agony. Jeremiah, the Old Testament prophet, spoke for all of us when he said: 'Is it nothing to you, all you who pass by? Behold and see if there is any sorrow like my sorrow.' There may well be clues in the lives and experiences of others about how we are feeling and what we are going through, but no one can really know how I am feeling at any given moment in bereavement. There is a deep kinship in grief, but there are no identical twins.

Grief is not an indulgence which is grudgingly permitted in our brittle, fun-orientated society. Although there is a deep and pervasive impatience with continuing grief which tends to feel that having taken the trouble to send off a sympathy card the person to whom we send it will soon settle down and within a week or two will be back to normal again. What we are dealing with in bereavement is amputation, and however we look at things, and whatever the circumstances, life never will be quite the same again, nor can it be. This does not mean that life stops or becomes intolerable, but it will forever be different.

Every generation seems to have its own taboos: for the Victorians it was sexuality, for our age it seems to be death. Though death is such a common feature of life, it is, in reality, the last thing we want to talk about. We find that it frequently causes embarrassment, and sometimes even fear. Much of this fear, of course, is due to ignorance, and is self-perpetuating. We fear death, so we do not talk about it; we shield our children from it, and, therefore, they too fear it the more. As a society our attitudes to death and dying are quite unhealthy.

C. S. Lewis, writing after the death of his wife, makes a very searching observation:

> An odd by-product of my loss is that I am aware of being an embarrassment to everyone I meet. At work, at the club, in the street, I see people, as they approach me, trying to make up their minds whether they'll 'say something about it' or not. I hate it if they do, and if they don't. Some funk it altogether. R has been avoiding me for a week. I like best the well brought-up young men, almost boys, who walk up to me as if I were a dentist, turn very red, get it over and then edge away to the bar as quickly as they decently can. Perhaps the bereaved ought to be isolated in special settlements like lepers.

But responding to the death of a loved one is not an option. It is painful and personal, natural and necessary. It cannot be avoided, nor ought it to be. Society in the past was much more realistic about grief than we are today. The question is sometimes asked and often dismissed: 'Can a man die of grief?' Yet the idea of 'dying of a broken heart' has an ancient history. In Dr Heberden's Bill listing the causes of death in London for the year 1657 we find:

Flox and Small Pox	–	835
Found dead in the streets, etc.	–	9
French Pox	–	25
Gout	–	8
Griefe	–	10
Griping and Plague in the Guts	–	466
Hang'd and made away 'emselves	–	24

Dr Joan Christison has an unpublished lecture on 'Grief Reaction' in which she writes:

Acute grief is a definite syndrome, with both physical and psychological manifestations, which may appear immediately after bereavement or may be delayed, exaggerated, or apparently absent. Bereavement itself may cause psychiatric emergencies, unless it is properly handled.

Even for those who have been long assured of the Christian hope and their eternal salvation the experience of being compelled to walk through the valley of the shadow of death often comes as an extremely painful, lonely and disturbing experience!

We need to know – whether anyone tells us or not – that it is permitted to grieve, whether I am a Christian or not. We need to hear the sound of Jesus weeping at the grave of His dear friend Lazarus. All kinds of reasons have been given why Jesus wept – that He saw more than His friend enshrouded in grave clothes; that He looked down the long corridor stretching through all history and all mortality; that He saw Eden and the primal pair at the end of the tunnel; that He wept not simply because Lazarus was dead, but that he had to die at all; that He wept for sin and for all the waste and tragedy that are sin's heritage. But the fact is that He did weep! Who can ever tell what stimulates the flow of weeping in the experience of death? Often with us, as with the Lord Jesus Christ, the real reasons scarcely present themselves and are certainly seldom analysed. One of the expressions of the reality of Jesus' humanity was that He burst into tears. The only place where this word (*edakrusem*) occurs in the New Testament is in this passage in John 11:35 – and it is a strong word!

Although tears are not always the best gauge of grief and a noisy hysterical funeral can sometimes be a shallow and superficial affair since many who cry easily are as likely to laugh with equal facility – yet tears have the ability to cleanse wounds that grief has inflicted and so healing can the more readily take place. We need strongly to challenge the pride which can often prevent weeping and we need to be convinced that there is no disgrace in tears!

Often well-meaning family or close friends, not quite knowing what to do and yet feeling they need to do something which is relevant will tell the bereaved to pull themselves together, and after a time speak with a strange assurance that 'you ought to be getting over it by now'. Unhappily mourning is treated as if it were a weakness, a self-indulgence, a reprehensible bad habit, instead of a psychological necessity. It is often more a commentary on our society rather than upon us when we are made to feel guilty about expressing our grief after the funeral is over. I want to say as clearly as possible that it is natural, right and permissible to grieve – and part of that process is weeping. Colin Murray Parkes in his excellent book *Bereavement: Studies of Grief in Adult Life* says:

> Newly bereaved people are often surprised and
> frightened by the sheer intensity of their emotions and
> imaginings after bereavement. Reassurance that they
> are not going mad, that such feelings are perfectly
> natural, and that crying does not mean a 'nervous
> breakdown' can be given explicitly, especially by an
> attitude which shows that the helper is not alarmed,
> frightened or even surprised.

So there is no need to feel embarrassed – you have permission to cry!

Catherine Marshall tells us that, on the death of her husband Peter with whom she had enjoyed a warm and happy marriage until his sudden and unexpected death at the age of 46 at 8.15 on a grey January morning, one of the lessons she learned was not to try to hide or steel her emotions. She says:

> Trying to force oneself to be brave will not heal the heart.
> This is hard for men who are trained to believe that

tears are the sign of weakness. But it is forever true that when the storms of life are savage, it is the tree that bends with the wind that survives. Tensing up, walling up the heart, damning up the tears, will inevitably mean trouble later on, perhaps years later. There is emotional release in letting the tears flow.

My first significant bereavement occurred when I was a young man of 19 – but it was not until over 30 years later that a retired naval captain and his wife gave me permission to cry – to my great surprise and relief I did! It was not that I had never cried before, but no one had ever said that I could without feeling guilty, alarmed or embarrassed.

Incidentally, it is sometimes necessary to have permission to stop grieving; that grieving has been done adequately and life can be picked up again and enjoyed without any feelings of guilt and with a clear conscience. Although this may seem mechanical and even objectionable, a pattern of grief can be formed which becomes a rigid structure and can frustrate any possibility of living freely again.

We need to have the ability and the opportunity to talk about our bereavement. In previous generations the natural processes of sex, birth and reproduction were scarcely mentioned in polite society whereas, death was spoken of freely, taken for granted and made the subject of normal conversation. In our age, however, death is not discussed in polite society, but we lay high premium on sex and eroticism. Stuart Barton Babbage in *The Mark of Cain* says:

> Our grandparents in their embarrassment and self-consciousness of the facts of birth, said that babies were found under gooseberry bushes, and we, in our self-consciousness over the facts of death, speak of 'passing on'.

So in our secularised, humanistic society death enjoys an almost universal taboo among topics of conversation. This places an inherent restriction upon our need to talk about our grief. Grief wants to be heard – and needs to be heard! In bereavement our whole world has suddenly gone topsy-turvy and the weird new landscapes need to be described. Memories need to be examined, lingered over, and discussed. Anton Chekhov depicts this need very powerfully in his classic short story, *The Lament*. Iona Potapov's son has died and no one will listen to Iona, and finally in his desperation he tries for relief by telling the whole story to his horse. That is quite a reflection on our society. Was this one reason why Jesus commended His mother and His beloved disciple John to each other's care from the Cross? Did He provide utterly unwearied ears that would listen as each poured out the innermost feelings and yearnings and hurts of the heart to the other? How sensitive Jesus was! How considerate! How realistic! How practical! You need to learn to talk about your grief (as others need to learn how to listen) in our embarrassed society!

It is helpful not only feeling free to cry and having the opportunity to talk, but also realising that there is a pattern to grief and a process which it needs to go through. Grief is not so much a state as a process, and as such it has different stages. These stages are not water-tight compartments, exclusive from each other, but they overlap and differ in sequence in different people. There are certain constants, however, of which we really need to be aware. Though the circumstances and outward displays may vary, the nature and pattern of grief is very similar in most cases. One helpful outline of the stages of grief is given by Jean Richardson, in her booklet *A Death in the Family*. She gives the following order: 1. Shock, often accompanied by physical feelings of weakness. 2. Numbness. 3. Struggle between fantasy and reality; the person may not be able to accept what has happened. 4. Feelings of guilt, panic or frenzy. 5. Depression. 6. Release, e.g. shedding tears. 7. Painful memories, but these can now be accepted. 8. Acceptance.

The importance of such an outline is not to provide a

rigid structure for the sequence of the process, but to give identifiable landmarks in the reality of grief where the currents are so strong that they can sweep us entirely away. These landmarks need to be identified not so that they can be avoided, but so that we can understand their presence and reality when we are confronted by them, and so are not taken by surprise. Let us set down some of these landmarks and consider them at least in part.

Shock. Often shock is characterised in the bereavement process by crying. Unfortunately crying has come to be accepted in our society as a sign of weakness. In our civilisation we detest weakness and so we are unhappy to witness the spectacle of tears. It would seem that we prefer silence, and we even assume that a person who adopts this attitude is 'coping' with the situation – often it can be the very reverse. Crying is merely a bodily function which releases tension – a tension which is almost impossible to analyse, but is being built up within the bereaved person. We should learn to respect that and not despise it.

I learned that my father had died very suddenly, though not unexpectedly, while I was working in Singapore. One of the Directors of the Mission I was working with telephoned me to say that he wanted to come round and see me right away. It was evening and the day's activities were over. I could not understand why he needed to come then – my mind began to race. As I waited at the door for him to arrive I became more and more anxious. My mind eventually locked in to the conviction that something must have happened at home. That conviction narrowed to the place that I felt it must be something in my family – one of the children perhaps! The seconds seemed like hours and the minutes as they passed like eternity. Every car that passed had an effect on my stomach. Eventually Denis arrived and asked if he could go with me to my room. He was calm and gentle and appeared to have everything under control. Maybe he simply wanted to discuss plans which could not wait until tomorrow!

148

We arrived in our room, where Anne was waiting, and I struggled to be very matter-of-fact, although everything within me wanted to scream out, 'Why are you here? There is something wrong isn't there?' Then Denis began very quietly to tell us that he had just received a 'phone call from home, and that he was sorry to tell me that my father had died. My heart went out to Denis since I had occasionally been in a similar position to him and been the bearer of unexpected and unwelcome news. I felt a deep gratitude to him for his gentleness and understanding and sensitivity and courtesy. He shared the brief details as he knew them, and explained that my brother would be contacting me direct in about two-and-a-half hours' time. He prayed with us both – and I appreciated that. In his simple prayer he verbalised what was in my heart, and I received the gracious ministry of God through it. Then Denis left!

We had arranged to meet two close friends for a meal that evening since we were on our way to the Philippines in the morning. It did not occur to me to alter the arrangement, and I felt that I was coping pretty well. After all, my father had been in indifferent health for some years; his heart condition had severely restricted his very energetic life; sometimes he was stricken with chest pains and became alarmingly breathless; he was after all, in his eighties; I had spoken with him on the telephone the night before I had left England for the Far East; I had written regularly to him while I had been gone; all these thoughts had surged through my mind. Anne, as always, was there with me in a much more significant way than physically – I could feel her love and tenderness and understanding. Her silence was eloquently healing – I knew she knew I knew!

Our friends arrived and we shared the news – they were so loving and sensitive – and they wanted to cancel the arrangements for the evening. I could see no reason at all for this. I had just closed the door behind us as we made our way to the restaurant for our meal, when I was suddenly, unexpectedly, publicly overwhelmed by tears. They shook me quite uncontrollably – and I felt so foolish and terribly embarrassed and exposed.

It is easy to say now that that was good and almost inevitable – but it did not seem good at that moment. But the process of grief had begun.

For others, however, the initial reaction to death is *numbness* and even denial. There sometimes will be a total inability to take the fact in that a loved one has died. It is a dream-like state, nightmarish in quality, and carries with it the feeling that he or she will wake up in the morning only to find things are they were. In normal circumstances that numbness will pass in a day or two. While it lasts, however, it is comparable to a kind of paralysis – the person is almost literally 'stricken' with grief. They have been 'struck' a blow, and so there is a time of inertia when thinking and even movement are slow, and an inability to cope with simple, routine, normal things. Sometimes there is the accompaniment of a feeling of shock that the 'normal' world around should continue on its busy way, and a sense of resentment that social life should be continuing. Periodically there will be waves of intense and almost intolerable longing for the loved one who has been 'lost'. Numbness will often manifest itself by sitting in silence and lethargy and disinterest and apathy to all that is happening both in the house and in the wider world.

Ritual mourning is often a great help in these early days, and should not be despised. John Hinton puts it:

The practice of mourning provides more than this socially approved catharsis of grief. It insists that the death has occurred, repeatedly demonstrating this fact over a few days so that the bereaved, whatever their state of mind, accept the painful knowledge, assimilate it, and begin to plan accordingly. Viewing the body and taking part in the funeral emphasise beyond all doubt that the person is really dead. The condolences, the discussion of the deceased in the past tense, the newspaper announcements, the public recognition of the death, all affirm the loss.

Until fairly recently in Scotland – certainly within my own lifetime – the 'kirking' of the mourners (a corporate act by a family of attending church after a set period of time subsequent to the death and sitting together in mourning clothes – black ties; black hats for the ladies; black armbands; etc.); the celebration of wakes; and eating elaborate meals after funeral services provided a catharsis of grief symptoms. These customs, however, are now dying out and, with funerals smaller, less personal, less communal, and more professionally organised, society generally and human psychology particularly has suffered. It would be difficult now to reverse the trend – and it would be unlikely that many would want to – but if these ceremonies did nothing else at least they insisted on the fact of death. They had a healing effect upon the scars made by grief. In 1967 Jeffrey Gorer, author of *Death, Grieving and Mourning in Contemporary Britain* pointed out that bereaved people no longer knew how they should behave unless they belonged to a religious group. Whether this is fair comment or not it may well be true that these groups practise ritual mourning with more ease than others.

In practical terms it is not always for the best to 'get it all over as quickly and with as little fuss as possible' – even though our inclinations would be towards doing just that.

Another of the landmarks in the process of grief is a tendency to *fantasy* – a denial of reality. It is not at all uncommon for the bereaved to half expect the door to open and the loved one to appear at his regular hour, for his favourite chair to be filled, as it has been for years. There is an irrational unbelief that the loved one has died and an unwillingness to accept the loss. Sometimes mourners pretend that death has not happened. They may well speak of the deceased as if he were still alive; they may prepare his bed for him; or set a table for a meal with his place as usual

151

as if he were coming home. They may speak of the deceased as 'just sleeping', or speak as if he will come to the house again, having gone on a short journey.

I remember visiting two sisters who lived together in a delightful little bungalow. They had had a wonderful family life together and now were the only unmarried ones who lived together in the family home. The passage of the years and failing health meant they had to move together into a nursing home. This they did, but lived in a double room with two single beds. Then one died after only a few days' real illness. I called several times subsequent to her death and the one who remained, looking in the direction of her sister's now empty bed, spoke of her sister as having had to go away and she did not know where she had gone or when she would return. She spoke very lovingly of her, but in a very matter of fact way. In those very early days insistence on the reality of the death of her sister seemed not only to be inappropriate, but quite impossible. It was a temporary experience, but nevertheless very real.

Aggression, strong and persistent, frequently is a part of the grief process. This will often assume various forms. It will be directed sometimes against the Christian minister. If the mourning family has little interest in spiritual matters, they may feel embarrassed at having to 'humble' themselves to ask for the assistance of an 'authoritative' person. In one study, *Exploring English Character,* Jeffrey Gorer discovered that in England about one-half of the population disclaims any religious belief and about one-half do not believe in an after-life. This creates all kinds of tensions when the reality of death has to be confronted and the fundamental questions of life have to be faced. Ignorance and confusion provide rich seed-beds for aggression. People begin to see themselves alone and impoverished and they are searching for an answer. Supremely, aggression can be directed against God: 'Why did God let this happen to me?' 'Why did God let that happen to him/her?' Deep within many human hearts is a sense that God is a retributive God.

Death is seen as a kind of punishment, not only to the deceased, but also to those who are left. In death, God has let us down! However, it is much easier and more plausible to direct this kind of aggression against another human being than against God – so 'God's representative', the minister or vicar or priest, will bear the brunt of it. In this same realm, a church fellowship may be criticised for having neglected the deceased ('. . . after all she did for the church in her younger days'). Surgeons may be censured for 'not having operated on time'. Doctors, too, are included in this strong attack for 'not having come when they were called'. Nurses are judged, often without any justification, for having 'neglected the patient'. However, supremely, in this phase it is God who is blamed, and however irrational it may be, it is against God that the real anger is directed.

It is very seldom that I have found *guilt* absent from the grief process. However confidently the bereaved person says that he has done all that he could do for the deceased – and that often with the fullest justification – there are few living relationships which in life reached such a stage of perfection that there were no flaws at all. As memories begin to stir there is an inevitable remembering of areas and incidents in the relationship which could have been handled much better than they were – the angry word; the unspoken word; the selfish action; the thoughtless attitude; the proud silence; the lack of consideration; and so on and on – it is endless!! This is compounded when there was some major quarrel or estrangement not long before death occurred. Sometimes a conviction even emerges that the quarrel or estrangement actually contributed to the death.

Not long ago I was counselling a woman – now married with two children of her own – who was convinced that she was responsible for her father's death because when she was a tiny little girl she insisted that he and not her mother get up out of bed to get her a drink in the night. I rather think that a tantrum might have accompanied the incident, although she did not say so! Her father died that night of a heart attack while in fact he was delivering the drink, and all these years she had felt guilty and full of remorse that she had caused his death.

It is part of the imperfection of our humanity that our relationships bear the marks of our sin – and often the closer and dearer these relationships are, the more obvious the flaws become, and so the more painful their memory in bereavement.

Only Jesus Christ can deal with our sin – and facing up to it; repenting of it; receiving His forgiveness and cleansing from it alone can remove it. It is no bad thing, however, to share with a trusted confidant that there were areas in the relationship which were not all that they might have been. It is of immeasurable strength when that person can accompany you to the only One who can forgive and remove sin – Jesus Christ.

In all of this – and for all of us – there needs to be a new appreciation that however final death undoubtedly seems; however close and warm and satisfying the relationship has been; however bleak and lonely and empty the future now appears without the company, the encouragement, or the security which the beloved one has brought; death is not the end; death is not the ultimate reality. That is a conviction which is not easily won!

Dietrich Bonhoeffer was put into the main Gestapo prison in the Prinz Albrechtstrasse in Berlin on the 5th October, 1944. Although fully aware of what he had to expect there, he was perfectly calm, saying goodbye to his friends as though nothing had happened. It was the following Spring – having been transferred to Buchenwald concentration camp and then to the concentration camp at Flossenburg because the Berlin prison had been destroyed in an air raid – that Bonhoeffer was hanged on the 9th April, 1945 by the Nazi SS Black Guards at the age of 39. A few days later Flossenburg was liberated by the Allies. All this happened at the same time as his brother Klaus and the husbands of his two sisters, Hans von Dohnanyi and

Rüdiger Schleicher, met their executions at the hands of the Gestapo in Berlin and in the concentration camp at Sachsenhausen. The guiding force in Bonhoeffer's life, underlying all that he did, worked and suffered for, was his faith in and his love for God, in whom he found reality, stability and peace. From his Christian faith came the breadth of vision which enabled him to separate the gold in life from the dross and to differentiate what was and what was not essential in the life of man. From that came his constancy of mind, persistency of purpose, love of suffering humanity, and of truth, justice and goodness. When he realised that his death was certain, and that others whom he loved were facing a similar event, he composed a poem in prison called *Stations on the Road to Freedom*. The last verse runs as follows:

Come now, solemnest feast on the road to eternal
    freedom,
Death, and destroy these fetters that bow, those walls
    that imprison
this our transient life, these souls that linger in
    darkness,
so that at last we see what is here withheld from our
    vision.
Long did we seek you, freedom, in discipline, action
    and suffering
Now that we die, in the fact of God Himself we behold
    you.

However hostile death may be — the ultimate enemy in fact — it is not the ultimate reality. The ultimate reality is life — with God or without Him. Death is the supreme festival on the road to freedom — or the station where we disembark in order to arrive at final liberty, in Bonhoeffer's words. It is only for the natural man, the man without God, without Christ, without hope and without grace that death is, in the words of John Donne:

A bloody conflict and no victory at last, a tempestuous sea and no harbour at last; a slippery height and no footing; a desperate fall and no bottom.

We need to die in order to live. We need to take our farewells from the land of the dying in order that we might enter into the land of the living.

John Bunyan has a marvellous description of Mr Valiant-for-Truth passing through the event of death:

> Then said he: 'I am going to my fathers, and though with great difficulty I am got thither, yet now I do not repent me of all the trouble I have been at to arrive where I am. My sword I give to him that shall succeed me in my pilgrimage, and my courage and skill to him that can get it. My marks and scars I carry with me, to be a witness for me that I have fought His battles who will now be my Rewarder.' When the day that he must go hence was come, many accompanied him to the riverside, unto which as he went he said: 'Death, where is thy sting?' And as he went down deeper he said: 'Grave, where is thy victory?' So he passed over and all the trumpets sounded for him on the other side.

Such is the Christian hope. Such is the ultimate Christian comfort in the face of death. The night must give way to the dawn and the darkness must give way to the light. The apparent finality of death must give way to the real fullness of resurrection. However bowed and broken our heart God wants to lift up our eyes from all the pain and hurt of parting to that glad morning of great reunion in the presence of Jesus Christ. The Christian Gospel alone enables us to comfort one another in this way in our bereavement.

Dr Peter Marshall, a Scotsman who was to become the Chaplain to the Senate of the United States, became well known, not only for his preaching, but also for his praying, prayed this prayer, which I now invite you to pray through your tears, bewilderment and loneliness:

Father, eyes blinded by the symbols of sorrow cannot see the stars. Even so, I, at this moment, can see nothing beyond my own grief.

I have been face to face with misery and loneliness in these days; with the strangeness of life and death that takes away a loved one and gives no explanation; with the mystery of a Providence I have tried to understand and cannot understand.

Thou, O Holy Spirit, Thou visitor in sorrow. Thou who art acquainted with human tears and broken hearts, sorely I need Thy help now.

Because my heart is sore, I have shut the door of my heart to my fellows, even to Thee. But I sense that withdrawal and the effort to dull my feelings is not the way toward healing. Help me now to dare to open my being wide to the balm of Thy loving Spirit, unafraid of any depth or height or intensity of overflowing emotion.

Thou hast promised to wipe away all tears from our eyes.

I ask Thee to fulfil that promise now.

Thou hast promised to bind up our wounded spirits.

I ask Thee to fulfil that promise now.

Thou hast promised to give us peace, not as the world gives, but in the midst of our trouble.

I ask Thee to fulfil that promise now.

Thou hast promised to be with us alway.

I therefore thank Thee that Thou art walking beside me every step of the way.

I put my hand in Thine, and walk on into the future, knowing that it will be a good future because Thou art in it. Amen.